How to Pray for Your Husband

Bless Your Husband Everyday

Nicole Perkins

ISBN: 978-1-62943-022-5
eBook ISBN: 978-1-62943-023-2

How to Pray for Your Husband

CONTENTS

Contents

How to Pray for Your Husband

Nicole Perkins

INTRODUCTION

Why Pray for Your Husband?

Throughout the Bible God uses marriage as a metaphor for the relationship he desires to have with His people. It has always been God's desire since the beginning to be in fellowship and deep communion with His creation. Husbands are commanded to love, honor, cherish, protect and provide for their wife as a representative of Christ. Wives are commanded to submit, obey, reverence, and respect their husband and to teach their children to do the same. Marriage is not a light thing and should not be entered into without a complete understanding of the responsibilities and roles that are required to sustain a marriage.

As a wife, there are many duties you have concerning your husband. You cook, provide a clean, peaceful home environment, attend to the children, and any number of things. However, your first duty to your husband is to pray for him. Once you begin to ask God to come to your husband's aid, everything else in his life and in your marriage will come together. Mark 10:7-9 says, "For this reason a man will leave his father and mother and be united to his wife, and the two will become one flesh. So they are no longer two, but one flesh. Therefore what God has joined together, let no one separate." God designed marriage to be an example of the type of relationship He wants the Church to have with Him. When you became born again, you joined yourself with Christ. This Christian life is about the process of becoming one with the Father through the Son by the power of the Holy Spirit. When you married your husband, you vowed to become one with him. The circumstances of life and temptations attempt to separate even the most devoted husbands and wives. However, daily prayers for your husband will help to ensure that what God has joined together can not be separated.

Daily prayer is especially important for newlyweds. The first year or two can be a difficult time of adjustment for some. The older you are when you marry, the longer you and your husband have had to get set in your ways of doing things. For a woman it can be hard to allow your husband to serve you and take over the things that you had become so accustomed to doing for yourself. A husband may find it hard to think about his wife and consider how his decisions will affect her. Marriage is a learned behavior. Be gracious and full of mercy toward one another, and in all things, pray.

When God made creation, he created the heavens, the earth, and every living thing and then He made man. Man was made in His image and was supposed to be His final creation. In Genesis 2:18, "The Lord God said, it's not good that man should be alone; I will make him a help meet for him." We know that the help meet was woman. She was created for the sole purpose of helping man. She was designed to help meet his needs for companionship, his physical needs and to give him purpose. A wife by definition is a woman who helps. The best way to help your husband is to be his one woman cheering section. You can uphold him daily, in prayer and help make his life easier. God sees the wife as an extension of the husband. So when he is blessed, you'll be blessed. When he is whole, you will reap the benefits. Now that you're convinced of the need to pray for your husband, let's look at how you should pray for him.

How to Pray for Your Husband

We all know we need to pray but we often don't pray because we don't know how. We either don't know how to begin or we don't feel we know the right words to say. The first thing to remember is that prayer is not a mysterious thing. It's as natural as breathing. Prayer is nothing more than a heartfelt conversation with God. Sometimes we don't pray because we don't feel worthy. We don't believe that the Almighty God will hear our prayers. This book was written to give you a simple format from which to pray for your husband. Each prayer in this book is broken down into three parts.

- A foundational Scripture
- A Petition or request made to God
- A statement of Gratitude

You'll begin by reading the foundational Scripture. Then you'll spend some time meditating on the words and asking the Holy Spirit to show you how the scripture can be applied to your situation. Once you have an understanding of the Scripture you'll begin to pray using the prayers in this book as a launching pad to make your own personal request. After spending some time interceding on behalf of your husband, you'll end your prayer by thanking God for hearing and answering. If your heart is still heavy, you can spend a prolonged time praising and worshiping God.

In Matthew chapter 6 Jesus gave a lesson on how to pray. Verses 5-7 say, "When you pray, you shall not be like the hypocrites. For they love to pray standing in the synagogues and on the corners of the streets, that they may be seen by men. But you, when you pray, go into your room, and when you have shut your door, pray to your Father who is in the secret place; and your Father who sees in secret will reward you openly. And when you pray, do not use vain repetitions as the heathen do. For they think they will be heard for their many words". Jesus makes it very clear that prayer is a personal matter between you and the Father. You don't have to be loud or long winded. All we need to do is simply, address our Father in heaven and make our request known.

There is power to be found in the secret place. Once you enter into His presence and release your burdens and make your request, things begin to change almost immediately. In the secret place you can exchange heaviness for joy, worry for peace, and confusion for confidence. Never underestimate what can happen when you take the time to get alone with God in a place of prayer. If you remain diligent to go into the secret place, God will reward you with insight and answered prayers.

Before you go into your place of prayer, try to discharge any negative emotions regarding the topic of prayer. If you're in distress or angry, you'll have a hard time praying effectively. When you feel this way, scream, cry, or go for a walk, play worship music; do whatever you must in order to find a place of peace. It's in the place of peace that you'll be able to focus on the Scriptures and hear what the Spirit of God has to say to you. Once your soul is at rest; your mind is at rest, then and only then will you be ready to pray.

How to Use this Book

I would suggest that you begin with section one. In the first section, you'll learn the foundational Scriptures concerning prayer. You'll also learn how to pray for yourself. If you're one of those people who thinks you are not worthy to pray, this section will help you get started. Lastly, this section contains prayers that you can pray daily over your husband. The remaining sections are divided by subjects. You can find the topic that concerns you and pray that prayer along with the daily prayers as needed. I've found that prayer is most effective when used as a preventative measure. Your husband may not have any career issues at this time. However, you can still pray that he be successful in his present field. That he becomes the best in his field and that people begin to seek him out for his knowledge. That he receives favor and promotion on his current job.

I recommend that you spend thirty minutes each day praying for your husband. If you already have a special time set aside for prayer, then add your husband to your prayer list. There is also a section that covers corporate prayer. These are prayers you can pray with your husband. When there are issues in the marriage, the best prayer will be a united prayer of agreement. Matthew 18:19-20 says, "Again I say unto you, That if two of you shall agree on earth as touching any thing that they shall ask, it shall be done for them of my Father which is in heaven. For where two or three are gathered together in my name, there am I in the midst of them. Your prayers for your husband shouldn't be a secret. He should know that you pray for him. He should be encouraged to pray for you and with you as well.

Many women find it difficult to pray with their husbands. If your husband is saved, he won't have any problem praying and agreeing with you about matters that concern your family. James 4:2-3 says, "You do not have because you do not ask. You ask and do not receive, because you ask amiss, that you may spend it on your pleasures. Wives need to be mindful at times how we approach our husbands with concerns. Sometimes we think we have asked for something when we have actually placed a demand. It's hard to require another person to do something when they have not been convinced of the benefits of doing so. If your husband is not one that is quick to pray, then you pray for him first. Ask God to burn a desire for communion with Him in your husband's heart. Share your desire to ask God to be an active partner in your marriage with your husband. Then ask him, if he would make some time to join you in prayer for the things that have been a concern in your marriage. If there are children in the marriage, you can also pray for them. When they are old enough they can join in the corporate family prayer. They need to know that in addition to mom and dad, they have a heavenly Father who loves them too.

1 John 4:8 says that God is love. True intercession is born from a place of intense love. Your love for your husband is what fuels your daily prayers for him. Love enables you to stand firm in your faith and know that in time the answer will come. Sometimes after many years of marriage, couples find that they don't feel the same way they once did. They haven't really fallen out of love, but rather, they are no longer functioning as one unit anymore. Just as love fuels prayer, continual

prayer will serve to fuel your love.

It is my prayer for you, that this book will lead you into a deeper relationship with your heavenly Father and your husband. I ask God to bless and enrich your marriage every day. As you commit to faithfully pray for your husband, I pray that God would knit your hearts together in love. You shall no longer be two individuals but one flesh. In the name of Jesus, Amen.

.

SECTION ONE

Establishing Your Prayer Life

I'd like for you to think of prayer as a shawl. Prayer is a shawl that goes over the head and covers the entire body. God has promised to encompass His people. He covers us in the shadow of His wings. When we retreat in prayer, it's like covering ourselves in the presence of God. When we pray for others we cover them as with a shield of protection and blessings. However, some of God's children are filled with shame over past failings and need to be restored. If you feel as if you can't talk to God because of something you've done or didn't do, be assured that God is waiting for you to come and lay it down. *Psalm 86:5-7 says, "For you, Lord, are good, and ready to forgive; and abundant in mercy to all those who call upon You. Give ear, O Lord, to my prayer; and attend unto my supplications. In the day of my trouble I will call upon you, for you will answer me."* We must start with receiving God's love, mercy, grace, and forgiveness in our own lives before we can pray for others. The only prayer that God won't hear is one that is not prayed in faith. *Hebrews 11:6 says, "But without faith it is impossible to please Him; for he that comes to God must believe that He is, and that He is a rewarder of those who diligently seek Him.*

Once you have prayed you must determine not to waiver in your confession of faith. You have to settle it in your heart and mind that God is who He says He is in His Word. You have to know that He will do what He has promised. The only way to pray with confidence is to study the Scriptures. The only way to study the Scriptures is to read and meditate on what you read. You may need to ponder a Scripture for hours or maybe days before you believe it. Believing is the key to receiving when it comes to God. In Mark 9:23 Jesus tells the man with the possessed son, *"If you can believe, all things are possible to him who believes."* At times you may need to ask Jesus to help your unbelief. When you meditate on the scripture and ask for understanding, you can also ask for the ability to believe what the Word says is true. Practice meditating on the Scriptures now.

James 1:5-7 If any of you lack wisdom, let him ask of God, who gives to all liberally and without reproach, and it will be given to him. But let him ask in faith, with no doubting, for he who doubts is like a wave of the sea driven and tossed by the wind. For let not that man suppose that he will receive anything from the Lord; he is a double-minded man, unstable in all his ways.

Now let's pray a prayer based on the Scriptures you've read thus far in this section. I'll start and you can finish it as the Holy Spirit leads you to pray.

Father God, I ask you for wisdom today concerning how I should pray for my husband. Your Word says that you give wisdom freely to all who ask and I'm asking You to reveal to me the areas in which my husband needs covering. I ask in faith knowing that Your word says that faith pleases you. I ask you to forgive me for not thinking to pray for my husband. I thank You God for being ever attentive to my prayers. I now ask that you … [This is where you pray for your husband]

To end the prayer, simply thank God for hearing and answering your request. You may also spend some time worshiping and praising God for Who He is in you life and in your marriage.

Foundational Scriptural Prayers

The following prayers are scriptural prayers that you can pray everyday. First pray them over yourself and then over your husband. Because your faith is the key ingredient to any prayer, you must first be in faith and cover yourself in prayer. Intercessory prayer can become taxing and stressful if you are always bringing the burdens of others before God and never unloading your own. The first section of prayers is designed to build your personal relationship with God. Once you are confident that you are in right standing and operating in faith you can successfully pray for your husband.

We don't have to wonder if God wants to bless us. The only question is can you believe that He will? Taking the time to build your own faith and renew your bond with God through Christ will give you the confidence to pray for your husband in any situation. I've selected Scriptures from the Old and New Testaments because I believe all of Scripture was given for our instruction. If you don't have a structured prayer time, try spreading your prayer out over the course of a day. Pray some in the morning, one during lunch or on a break and the rest at night before bed.

It may also be beneficial to start a prayer journal. A simple notebook is all you need. When you sit down to pray write the date and jot down the prayers you prayed. Write down any impressions you may get while in prayer. What most people forget is that prayer is a conversation. Once you finish speaking, you should stop and listen to what God has to say to you. When He speaks, write it down. When you get answers to prayers, find the entry where you first prayed the prayer and write the date and how God answered. In time, your prayer journal will become a list of all the blessings of God in your life.

Attempting to do something as monumental as marriage, without God is like trying to paddle a boat upstream. You work hard and try and try but your best will never be good enough. Daily prayer is an invitation for God to get involved in your life. Once He is active, you'll be able to follow His direction. No more fighting the current, you'll simply go with the flow. As you develop this practice of daily prayer, believe that God will give you exactly what you need for each day.

Faith in God

Numbers 23:19 God is not a man, that He should lie, nor a son of man, that He should repent. Has he not said, and will He not do? Or has He spoken, and will He not make it good?

Prayer: Father God, I know that You alone are God. You are not like man; You are able to back up every word that You have spoken. I thank You that You will do everything You have said You would do for me and my family …

2 Samuel 22:2-4 The Lord is my rock and my fortress and my deliverer; the God of my strength, in whom will I trust; My shield and the horn of my salvation, My stronghold and my refuge; My Savior, You save me from violence. I will call upon the Lord, who is worthy to be praised; so shall I be saved from my enemies.

Prayer: Father God, I thank you today for being my deliverer. You are my strength and I trust in You and Your power to save and keep me from all danger. I will trust You with my life, my marriage, my children …

Mark 11:22-26 Jesus answered and said to them, "Have faith in God, For assuredly, I say to you, whoever says to this mountain, 'Be removed and be cast into the sea,' and does not doubt in his heart but believes that those things which he says will be done, he will have whatever he says. Therefore I say to you, whatever you ask for when you pray, believe that you receive them, and you will have them. And whenever you stand praying, if you have anything against anyone, forgive him that your Father in heaven may also forgive you your trespasses."

Prayer: Father God, I declare my complete faith in You and Your ability to give me whatever I say. I also believe that whatever I ask for in faith, will be given to me. Father, I forgive _____ for _____ and I ask that you also forgive me of my trespasses against Your will ...

Hebrews 10:20-23 Therefore, brethren, having boldness to enter the Holiest by the blood of Jesus, by a new and living way which He consecrated for us through the veil that is, His flesh, and having a High Priest over the house of God, let us draw near with a true heart in full assurance of faith, having our hearts sprinkled from an evil conscience and our bodies washed with pure water. Let us hold fast the confession of our hope without wavering, for He who promised is faithful.

Prayer: Father God, I know You are faithful and will keep Your promise to me. I draw near to You today with a true heart fully assured and full of faith. I thank You for the blood of Jesus which has cleansed me and made me righteous in Your sight. I enter boldly into the secret place today and ask that You would ...

1 John 5:14-15 Now this is the confidence we have in Him, that if we ask anything according to His will, He hears us. And if we know that He hears us, whatever we ask, we know that we have the petitions we have asked of Him.

Prayer: Father God, I've read Your Word and ask You to reveal Your will to me that I may pray with confidence. I thank You Father that when I pray according to Your will, you hear me and grant my request ...

Prayers that Build your Faith

Isaiah 30:18-19 "Therefore the Lord will wait, that He may be gracious to you; and therefore He will be exalted, that He may have mercy on you. For the Lord is a God of justice; blessed are all those who wait on Him."

Prayer: Father God, I come to You today and I ask You for mercy. Be gracious toward me as I exercise my faith to pray. I will wait on You daily in the secret place of prayer. I wait for You to reveal truth and to make Your purposes known to me concerning my marriage. Be exalted God, in our home, in our relationship ...

Luke 11:9-13 "So I say to you, ask and it will be given you; seek, and you will find; knock, and it will be opened to you. For everyone who asks; receives and he who seeks; finds, and to him who knocks it will be opened. If a son asks for bread from any father among you, will he give him a stone? Or if he asks for a fish, will he give him a scorpion? If you then, being evil, know how to give good gifts to your children, how much more will your heavenly Father give the Holy Spirit to those who ask Him?"

Prayer: Father God, I ask for and seek the Holy Spirit today. The Holy Spirit is a good gift that I need in order to pray Your word. By Your Spirit I will receive discernment, revelation, and guidance on how to pray for …

Philippians 1:9 "And this I pray, that your love may abound still more and more in knowledge and all discernment, that you may approve the things that are excellent, that you may be sincere and without offense till the day of Christ, being filled with the fruits of righteousness which are by Jesus Christ, to the glory and praise of God."

Prayer: Father God, may Your love abound in my heart today as I come to You in this time of prayer. I ask that You would give me knowledge and discernment for the challenges I face today …

Philippians 4:6-7 "Be anxious for nothing, but in everything by prayer and supplication, with thanksgiving, let your request be made known to God; and the peace of God, which surpasses all understanding, will guard your hearts and minds through Christ Jesus."

Prayer: Father God, I come to You today to receive Your peace. Your peace is a peace that surpasses all of my understanding and will keep my heart from fainting and guard my mind from fear. I will not be anxious in my prayers today, but rather I give You thanks that my requests will be heard. I exercise my faith today for …

Prayers of Consecration

Psalm 66: 18 "If I regard iniquity in my heart, the Lord will not hear."

Prayer: Father God, I release any iniquity that may be in heart. I repent of any sins. Things I've done as well as things I've neglected to do. I come to You today and ask that You search my heart and reveal anything that needs to be removed. I need You

to hear me concerning …

Psalm 143:1-2, 5-10 Hear my prayer, O Lord, Give ear to my supplication! In Your faithfulness answer me, and in Your righteousness. Do not enter into judgment with Your servant. For in Your sight no one living is righteous. I remember the days of old; I meditate on all Your works; I muse on the work of Your hands. I spread out my hands to You; My soul longs for You like a thirsty land. Answer me speedily, O Lord; My spirit fails! Do not hide Your face from me, Lest I be like those who go down into the pit. Cause me to hear Your loving kindness in the morning, for in You do I trust; cause me to know the way in which I should walk, for I lift up my soul to You. Deliver me, O Lord, from my enemies; in You I take shelter, teach me to do Your will, for You are my God; Your Spirit is good. Lead me in the Land of uprightness.

Prayer: Father I lift my soul up to you today. Teach me your ways that I may walk in them. I declare that You are my God, I am Your servant. Teach me to do Your will oh God. I thank You for Your faithfulness towards me and family. I meditate today on all that You've all ready done for us …

John 14:12-17 "Most assuredly, I say to you, he who believes in Me, the works that I do he will do also; and greater works than these he will do, because I go to My Father. And whatever you ask in My name, that I will do, that the Father may be glorified in the Son. If you ask anything in My name, I will do it. If you love Me, keep My commandments. And I will pray the Father, and He will give you another Helper, that He may abide with you forever – the Spirit of truth, whom the world cannot receive, because it neither see Him nor knows Him; but you know Him, for He dwells with you and will be in you."

Prayer: Father I thank you that Your Spirit dwells in me. I believe in Jesus and the works He has done in my life. I ask You to show me the greater works You have for me to do that You may be glorified in my life. I love You Lord and it is my desire to keep your commandments. In the name of Jesus I ask …

1 John 3:18-24 "My little children, let us not love in word or in tongue, but in deed and in truth. And by this we know that we are in the truth, and shall assure our hearts before Him. For if our hearts condemns us, God is greater than our heart, and knows all things. Beloved, if our heart does not condemn us, we have confidence toward God. And whatever we ask we receive from Him, because we keep His commandments and do those things that are pleasing in His sight. And this is His commandment; that we should believe on the name of His Son Jesus Christ and love one another, as He gave us commandment. Now he who keeps His commandments abides in Him and He in him. And by this we know that He abides in us, by the Sprit whom He has given us."

Prayer: Father it is my desire to keep Your commandments and to abide in You today. I thank You that Your Spirit abides in me through Jesus Christ. I desire to be pleasing in Your sight. I want to walk in confidence toward You God and my heart not be condemned. Teach me to love in deed and truth so my heart may be assured in Your presence ...

Now that you have gotten some practice praying for yourself, the remainder of this book can be used as a topical book of prayers. Once you find the topic that you need to pray about, spend some time reading through the Scriptures in that section. Meditate on the meaning of the Scriptures and ask the Holy Spirit for understanding when necessary. Starter prayers have been provided if nothing comes to you right away. However, once you have spent time meditating on the Scripture, feel free to just start talking with God about what's in your heart or on your mind.

This book was written as a guide. It serves as a reminder that it's important to pray in faith and believe that God is able to keep His promises. There is no formula that you can follow that will guarantee your success. However, the practice of reading God's Word and praying according to His Word will get results. As you make praying for your husband a priority, God will begin to work on his heart, deliver his mind, heal his body, and prosper him in everyway. Matthew 24:35 says, "Heaven and earth will pass away, but My words will by no means pass away." When you pray know that you have God's word on it. Whenever thing else fails, the Word of God will always stand.

I pray that during your time of daily prayer, you would grow stronger in your faith and trust in God and His Word. I ask that God will give you a special grace to pray for your husband every day without fail. As you spend time meditating of the Word of God, I pray that the Scriptures will come alive in your heart and mind. I ask that God would continue to knit you and your husband's hearts together in love. Amen.

SECTION 2

Praying for Your Husband's Spirit

The first area to intercede on behalf of your husband is his spirit. We are spirit first, and so any lasting change will need to take place first in the realm of the spirit. If you were a Christian when you got married, odds are you married a believer. However, you may have come to Christ after marriage. If that is your situation, you can take time to pray for your husband's salvation. According to 1 Corinthians 7 your prayers can turn the heart of your husband. But keep in mind that he will have to make a confession of faith for himself. Romans 10:9, makes it clear that one must confess with their own mouth and believe in their own heart. As a wife, you have been empowered by the Holy Spirit to pray and ask God to turn your husband's heart. This is an awesome responsibility, which no wife should ever take lightly. Your husband, as the head of the household can lead your family aright or astray. This is why God gave him you, and has called you to pray for him.

2 Corinthians 6:14 says, "Don't be unequally yoked together with unbelievers. For what fellowship has righteousness with lawlessness? And what communion has light with darkness?" This is an admonition not to marry an unbeliever, but it is not necessarily grounds for divorce. Yes, marriage with an unbeliever may be hard, especially if he is not open to idea of God. You are on the one hand told to submit to your husband. But on the other hand are not required to follow him in unrighteousness or to suffer abuse. Remember that you as a wife are called to help your husband. For some, that help begins with introducing him to Christ. Once saved, your husband will need your continued prayers and support as he begins to mature in the things of God and learns what it means to be a godly husband. As you know, from your own salvation experience, this is a process that can take years. But remain patient and in time you will see the fruit of your devotion to prayer in your husband's life.

In addition to prayer, you may also need to seek counseling as well. A good Christian counselor can help the two of you keep things in perspective, by being an objective observer who can show you the things you have overlooked. Newlyweds should not be ashamed to ask for help. Seek counsel whenever you find yourself at a cross roads and don't know what to do. *Proverbs 15:22 Without counsel, plans go awry, but in the multitude of counselors they are established.* Find an older couple that can serve as mentors for you and your husband. You may want to seek out an older married woman who can counsel you in how to love your husband as he goes through the process.

Salvation

2 Corinthians 4:3-6 But even if our gospel is veiled, it is veiled to those who are perishing, whose minds the god of this age has blinded, who do not believe, lest the light of the gospel of the glory of Christ, who is the image of God, should shine on them. For we do not preach ourselves, but Christ Jesus the Lord, and ourselves your bondservants for Jesus' sake. For it is God who commanded light to shine out of darkness, who has shone in our hearts to give the light of knowledge of the glory of God in the face of Jesus Christ.

Prayer: Lord God, open my husband's eyes to the gospel of Jesus Christ. I ask that the veil be removed from his eyes that he might see Jesus. God I command Your light to shine in his darkness ...

Colossians 4:2-4 Continue earnestly in prayer, being vigilant in it with thanksgiving; meanwhile praying also for us, that God would open to us a door for the word, to speak the mystery of Christ for which I am also in chains, that I may make it manifest, as I ought to speak. Walk in wisdom toward those who are outside, redeeming the time. Let your speech always be with grace, seasoned with salt, that you may know how you ought to answer each one.

Prayer: Father I ask You to open a door for Your word in my husband's life. Would You use me to make Jesus real to him? Give me wisdom and the words to speak concerning salvation ...

Hebrews 7:25 Therefore He is also able to save to the uttermost those who come to God through Him, since He always lives to make intercession for them.

Prayer: I thank You Jesus that You are able to totally save anyone who comes to God through You. As I intercede on behalf on my husband I pray that You would also make intercession for

him …

2 Peter 3:9 The Lord is not slack concerning His promises, as some count slackness, but is longsuffering toward us, not willing that any should perish but that all would come to repentance.

Prayer: I thank You Father that You are not slack concerning Your promises. You promised that You would save whole households. I thank You that it is not Your will that anyone should perish before they come to You and repent …

Maturity

1 Corinthians 13:11 When I was a child, I spoke as a child, I understood as a child, I thought as a child; but when I became a man, I put away childish things.

Prayer: Father, I thank You for the man You have given me. I acknowledge that he is no longer a child but a man. It is my prayer that he would put away all childish things …

Galatians 2:20 I have been crucified with Christ; it is no longer I who live, but Christ lives in me; and the life which I now live in the flesh I live by faith in the Son of God, who loved me and gave Himself for me.

Prayer: Father I pray that Christ would live and reign in my husband's life. May he experience the love of Christ and live by faith …

Galatians 5: 24-26 and those who are Christ's have crucified the flesh with its passions and desires. If we live in the Spirit, let us also walk in the Spirit. Let us not become conceited, provoking one another, envying one another.

Prayer: Father I pray that You would teach my husband what it means to crucify the flesh. Show him how to walk daily in the Spirit …

Ephesians 4:14-15 That we should no longer be children, tossed to and fro and carried about with every wind of doctrine, by the trickery of men, in the cunning craftiness of deceitful plotting, but, speaking the truth in love, may grow up in all things into Him who is the head – Christ.

Prayer: Father I pray that my husband would not chase after every doctrine or be tricked by men concerning the truth of Your

word. I pray that he would grow up into the things of Christ …

1 Thessalonians 3:12-13 And may the lord make you increase and abound in love to one another and to all, just as we do to you, so that He may establish your hearts blameless in holiness before our God and Father at the coming of our Lord Jesus Christ with all His Saints.

Prayer: Father I pray that my husband would abound in love toward all men. Establish his heart in holiness …

Wisdom

Proverbs 1:5 A wise man will hear and increase learning, a man of understanding will attain wise counsel.

Prayer: I thank You Father that You've given my husband wisdom that he may hear and increase his learning. I ask that You'd give him understanding of when to seek wise counsel …

1 Corinthians 2:9-10,12 But as it is written: "Eye has not seen, nor ear heard, nor have entered into the heart of man the things which God has prepared for those who love Him. But God has revealed them to us through His Spirit. For the Spirit searches all things, yes, the deep things of God. Now we have received, not the spirit of the world but the Spirit who is from God, that we might know the things that have been freely given to us by God.

Prayer: Father, I thank You that You have given us Your Holy Spirit that we might know the things You have prepared for us. Reveal some things by Your Spirit to my husband today concerning …

Colossians 1:9-12 For this reason we also, since the day we heard it, do not cease to pray for you, and to ask that you may be filled with the knowledge of His will in all wisdom and spiritual understanding; that you may walk worthy of the Lord, fully pleasing Him, being fruitful in every good work, and increasing in the knowledge of God; strengthened with all might, according to His glorious power, for all patience and longsuffering with joy; giving thanks to the Father who has qualified us to be partakers of the inheritance of the saints in the light.

Prayer: Father, I'll never cease to pray for my husband. I pray that he would be filled with the knowledge of Your will in all wisdom. Give him spiritual understanding of how to walk in a way that is worthy of You Lord …

James 1:5 If any of you lack wisdom, let him ask of God, who give to all liberally and without reproach, and it will be given to him.

Prayer: Father, I ask You to give my husband wisdom concerning _____. Speak to his heart today and give understanding ...

Obedience

Deuteronomy 12:28 Observe and obey all these words which I command you, that it may go well with you and your children after you forever, when you do what is good and right in the sight of the Lord your God.

Prayer: I thank You Father that You have promised to protect our family when we do what is good in Your sight. We desire to do Your will and to obey Your words and follow Your commandments, God ...

Isaiah 1:19-20 If you are willing and obedient, you shall eat the good of the land; but if you refuse and rebel, you shall be devoured by the sword.

Prayer: I pray that my husband would be willing and obedient when it comes to obeying Your Word. I thank You, God that You promised to reward us for our obedience to You. May he receive the good You have for him once he surrenders to You ...

Proverbs 16:9 A man's heart plans his way, but the Lord directs his steps.

Prayer: Lord, God I ask You to direct my husbands steps today. As he goes about his daily business be with him. Lead and guide him in all things. Speak to his heart and convince him that Your ways are best ...

Matthew 7:24-25 Therefore whoever hears these sayings of Mine, and does them, I will liken him to a wise man who built his house on the rock; and the rain descended, the floods came, and the winds blew and beat that house; and it did not fall, for it was founded on the rock.

Prayer: Father, I pray that my husband would be like the wise man who built his house on the rock. I pray that he would be

quick to obey so that no circumstance can destroy the house he is building because it is founded on the rock. It is founded on Your truth and done in a way that pleases You ...

1 Peter 1:13-16 Therefore gird up the loins of your mind, be sober, and rest your hope fully upon the grace that is to be brought to you at the revelation of Jesus Christ; as obedient children, not conforming yourselves to the former lusts, as in your ignorance; but as He who called you is holy, you also be holy in all your conduct, because it is written, "Be holy, for I am holy."

Prayer: Father I pray that my husband would learn to rest his hopes fully upon your grace today. Give him a revelation of Jesus Christ and what He has done for us all on the cross. I pray that my husband would not follow after his former lusts but rather seek holiness in everything ...

Forgiveness

Luke 6:36-37 Therefore be merciful, just as your Father is also merciful. "Judge not, and you shall not be judged. Condemn not and you shall not be condemned. Forgive, and you will be forgiven.

Prayer: Father I pray that my husband would be a man of mercy, just as You Father are merciful. That he would not be judgmental or condemning, but ever loving and forgiving ...

Luke 17: 3-4 Take heed to yourselves. If your brother sins against you, rebuke him; and if he repents, forgive him. And if he sins against you seven times in a day, and seven times in a day returns to you, saying, 'I repent,'' you shall forgive him.

Prayer: Father, I pray that my husband would be known as one who forgives. That he can forgive those who sin against him, even those who repeatedly abuse him. Let him walk in forgiveness daily ...

1 John 1:9 If we confess our sins, He is faithful and just to forgive us our sins and to cleanse us from all unrighteousness.

Prayer: Lord, God I thank You that when we confess our sins You are always faithful and just to forgive us. I pray that as my husband comes to You and confesses any sins and that You cleanse him today ...

If you are not in a church where the Word of God is preached, you may want to pray about whether you need to find a new church. A marriage can not succeed in a vacuum. You and your husband will need to be surrounded by a body of believers who can model the life of Christ for you. The saying goes, it take a village to raise one child. Well I would say that it takes a village to support one marriage. If your husband has turned away from God or maybe has never accepted him, you may feel alone in your marriage. But you are never alone because Your heavenly Father is with you always. Our pastor and our church family serve as reminders of God's love and encourage us in our faith.

The harsh reality is you may not be able to directly lead your husband to the Lord. 1 Corinthians 3:6-10 illustrates how when it comes to sharing the Gospel, one plants, another waters, but God gives the increase. Verse 9 calls us fellow workers with God. So your part may be to plant the seed or to water a seed planted by others. Know that at any time God can and will send the right person across your husband's path that can lead him to confess that Jesus is Lord.

I pray that you would grow in patience and understanding with your husband as you pray for the renewing of his spirit. I pray that the spirit of faith would arise and be big in your heart. Know that when no on else seems to care or understand, God cares and He knows exactly what you are going through. Romans 14:11 says, "For it is written: as I live, says the Lord, every knee shall bow to Me, and every tongue shall confess of God." I pray that you would learn to rest and find peace in knowing that every knee includes your husband. I ask that God would send forth laborers to preach and to teach the Word of God to your husband that he may hear and be saved. Once saved that he might be filled with the Holy Spirit who will enable him to live a godly life. Amen.

SECTION 3

Praying for Your Husband's Mind

The battle for a man is always won or lost in his mind. The Scriptures tell us to renew our minds if we want to find joy, happiness and peace. In this section you will pray for the Lord to keep your husband's mind. You will pray for his emotional stability and thought life. Much of the tension you may face in your marriage will be a result of things that one of you has not resolved in your mind. Ephesians 4:23 says, *"that we must be renewed in the spirit of our mind."* This changing of the mind helps us to live in righteousness and holiness as God intended.

Under stress and a tormented mind can manifest in a number of unhealthy ways. Stress can cause rapid weight loss or gain, insomnia, problems with digestion and depression. In your time of prayer, ask God to show you if your husband is under stress or needs emotional healing. Your kind words and loving touch can go a long way toward lightening his burden. In big ways and small ways, remind him often that you are in his corner. Become a good listening ear, so that he knows he can share concerns with you. Then take those concerns to God in prayer.

When the enemy of our souls attacks, he often goes straight for the mind. If he can get us to doubt God's promises then, he wins. Speak and pray the Word of God always over the situation. Once you have prayed, turn it over and let it go. The letting go is actually the harder part. We all live under the illusion that we have control over what happens to us. The reality is that we have very little control over what happens. What we can control is how we respond to what happens to us. Mental illness is a result of the brain's inability to process information correctly. As a result a person experiencing a mental break will be irrational and not respond to things in the way the average person without a mental illness would. If your husband is dealing with mental illness, you may need to seek counseling in addition to praying for him.

Emotional Health

Psalm 27:13 I would have lost heart, unless I had believed that I would see the goodness of the Lord in the land of the living.

Prayer: May my husband never lose heart. Father, I pray he would believe to see Your goodness every day for the rest of his life …

Psalm 55:22 Cast your burden on the Lord, and he shall sustain you; He shall never permit the righteous to be moved.

Prayer: Father God, by Your Spirit, teach my husband to cast every burden on the Lord. Only You are able to sustain him. I thank You, Lord that You will never permit the righteous to be moved …

Proverbs 16:2-3 All the ways of a man are pure in his own eyes, but the Lord weighs the spirits. Commit your works to the Lord, and your thoughts will be established.

Prayer: Father, I pray that my husband will commit all of his works to You. Establish his thoughts Lord as they begin to line up with Your Word. Open his eyes to the areas in which his thoughts need to be changed …

Romans 12:1-2 I beseech you therefore, brethren, by the mercies of God, that you present your bodies a living sacrifice, holy, acceptable to God, which is your reasonable service. And do not be conformed to this world, but be transformed by the renewing of your mind, that you may prove what is that good and acceptable and perfect will of God.

Prayer: Lord God, I pray that my husband would not be conformed to this world, but that he would be transformed as he renews his mind in Your Word. As his mind becomes renewed, I pray that he would be able to discern Your will for his life …

2 Corinthians 10:4-5 For the weapons of our warfare are not carnal but mighty in God for pulling down strongholds, casting down arguments and every high thing that exalts itself against the knowledge of God, bringing every thought into captivity to the obedience of Christ.

 Prayer: Lord God, I pray that my husband will learn how to do warfare. Teach him to cast down arguments and anything that tries to take Your place in his life. May he learn to take every thought captive ...

Stress

Psalm 23:1-3; 6 The Lord is my Shepherd; I shall not want. He makes me to lie down in green pastures; He leads me beside the still waters. He restores my soul; He leads me in the paths of righteousness for His name's sake. Surely goodness and mercy shall follow me all the days of my life; and I will dwell in the house of the Lord forever.

 Prayer: Lord God, I worship You and thank you for being our Shepherd. We shall not want for anything in this life. I ask You to restore my husband's soul today. Father lead him in the paths of righteousness. May goodness and mercy follow him the rest of the days of his life ...

Matthew 6:25-27; 33-34 Therefore I say to you, do not worry about your life, what you will eat or what you will drink; nor about your body, what you will put on. Is not life more than food and the body more than clothing? Look at the birds of the air, for they neither sow nor reap nor gather into barns; yet your heavenly Father feeds them. Are you not of more value than they? Which of you by worrying can add one cubit to his stature? But seek first the kingdom of God and His righteousness, and all these things shall be added to you. Therefore do not worry about tomorrow, for tomorrow will worry about its own things. Sufficient for the day is its own trouble.

 Prayer: I thank you Father that we are of more value than the birds of the air and the flowers of the field. We will seek first Your kingdom God and Your righteousness and watch as You give us everything we have asked for. Show my husband Your provision in a mighty way today so that he won't worry about ...

Matthew: 11:28-29 Come to Me, all you who labor and are heavy laden, and I will give you rest. Take My yoke upon you and learn from Me, for I am gentle and lowly in heart, and you will find rest for your souls.

 Prayer: Father we come to you today to lay down our heavy burdens in exchange for Your rest. My husband needs to find rest for his soul today ...

Romans 8:31; 35-36; 37-39 What then shall we say to these things? If God is for us, who can be against us? Who shall separate us from the love of Christ? Shall tribulation, or distress, or persecution, or famine, or nakedness, or peril, or sword? Yet in all these things we are more than conquerors through Him who loved us. For I am persuaded that neither death nor life, nor angels nor principalities nor powers, nor things present nor things to come, not height nor depth, nor any other created thing, shall be able to separate us from the love of God which is in Christ Jesus our Lord.

Prayer: I thank You Father God that nothing can ever separate us from Your Love. I declare that no matter what we go through we are more than conquerors through You …

Philippians 4: 6-8 Be anxious for nothing, but in everything by prayer and supplication, with thanksgiving, let your request be made known to God; and the peace of God, which surpasses all understanding, will guard your hearts and minds through Christ Jesus. Finally, brethren, whatever things are true, whatever things are noble, whatever things are just, whatever things are lovely, whatever things are of a good report, if there is any virtue and if there is anything praiseworthy – meditate on these things.

Prayer: I come against all anxiety in the Name of Jesus. I bring all our concerns to You in prayer today. I make it known today that my husband has been experiencing stress and I ask You to give him peace. He needs Your peace God to guard his heart and his mind …

Philippians 4:12-13; 19 I know how to be abased, and I know how to abound. Everywhere and in all things I have learned both to be full and to be hungry, both to abound and to suffer need. I can do all things through Christ who strengthens me. And my God shall supply all your need according to His riches in glory by Christ Jesus.

Prayer: Father our faith has been tried as of late, and we have learned what it means to be full and to be hungry. We have had abundance and have been in lack. Strengthen my husband's heart, Lord and remind him that He can do all things in You. I thank You God that You will supply all of our needs. I ask today for …

Fear

1 Chronicles 28:20-21 Be strong and of good courage, and do it; do not fear nor be dismayed, for the Lord God – my God- will be with you. He will not leave you nor forsake you, until you have finished all the work for the service of the house of the Lord.

Prayer: Father I pray that my husband would be strong and

very courageous today, that he would not fear or be dismayed because You are with him. I thank you God that You will never leave him nor forsake him ...

Psalm 34:4 I sought the Lord, and He heard me, and delivered me from all my fears.

Prayer: I'm seeking after You today, Lord. I ask that You would hear and deliver my husband from all of his fears. He has expressed the following fears _____ and I ask You to deliver him from each and every one ...

Psalm 46:1-2 God is a refuge and strength, a very present help in trouble. Therefore we will not fear.

Prayer: God be a refuge for my husband today. Be his strength. Help him in this time of trouble. We will not fear because ...

2 Timothy 1:7 For God has not given us a spirit of fear, but of power and of love and of a sound mind.

Prayer: I thank You God that You have not given us a spirit of fear. Release Your power and Your love today Lord. May my husband receive soundness of mind as he is filled with more of You ...

1 Peter 5:7 Casting your care upon Him, for he cares for you.

Prayer: Father I thank You that You care for my husband. I pray that he would cast every care on You today ...

1 John 4:18 There is no fear in love; but perfect love cast out fear, because fear involves torment. But he who fears has not been made perfect in love.

Prayer: Father God, I pray that we be made perfect in love toward You and towards one another. I ask that You would cast out all fear and torment that my husband may feel and make him perfect in love ...

Anger

Psalm 19:11 The discretion of a man makes him slow to anger, and his glory is to overlook a transgression.

Prayer: Father I ask that You by Your Spirit would teach my husband how to overlook transgressions ...

Psalm 37:8 Cease from anger, and forsake wrath; do not fret – it only causes harm.

Prayer: God I ask that You help my husband to cease from

anger today. I pray that he would forsake wrath and not fret ...

Proverbs 15:1 A soft answer turns away wrath, but a harsh word stirs up anger.
Prayer: Father help me to remember to answer softly to turn away all wrath. I pray that my husband would refrain from harsh words that stir up anger ...

Proverbs 16: 32 He who is slow to anger is better than the mighty, and he who rules his own spirit than he who takes a city.
Prayer: Father I ask that You by Your Spirit would teach my husband how to rule his own spirit ...

James 1:19-20 So then, my beloved brethren, let every man be swift to hear, slow to speak, slow to wrath; for the wrath of man does not produce the righteousness of God.
Prayer: Father I ask that You would teach my husband to be swift to hear, slow to speak, and slow to wrath. Your word says that wrath does not produce righteousness ...

Patience

Psalm 37:4-5;7 Delight yourself also in the Lord, and He shall give you the desires of your heart. Commit your way to the Lord, trust also in Him, and He shall bring it to pass. Rest in the Lord, and wait patiently for Him.
Prayer: Father God, we delight ourselves in You today. I thank You that as my husband commits his ways to You, all the things that he desires will come to pass. Teach him how to wait and to rest in You today ...

Isaiah 40:31 But those who wait on the Lord shall renew their strength; they shall mount up with wings like eagles, they shall run and not be weary, they shall walk and not faint.
Prayer: Father God You promise to renew our strength if we would only wait on You. Teach us how to wait. I pray for a lifting of any weariness my husband has experienced. I pray that he would walk and not faint ...

Hebrews 6:1-12 And we desire that each one of you show the same diligence to the full assurance of hope until the end, that you do not become sluggish, but imitate those who through faith and patience inherit the promises.
Prayer: Father I pray that my husband would remain diligent even during trying times. May he continue in faith and patience and inherit the promises ...

James 1:2-4 My brethren, count it all joy when you fall into various trials, knowing that the testing of your faith produces patience. But let patience have its perfect work, that you may be perfect and complete, lacking nothing.

Prayer: Father lately my husband's faith has been tested. Teach him how to find joy in the middle of it. May this current testing produce patience in him ...

Temptation

Matthew 26:41 Watch and pray, lest you enter into temptation. The spirit indeed is willing but the flesh is weak.

Prayer: Teach my husband how to watch and pray today Father God so he will not enter into temptation. When his spirit is willing to obey but his flesh is weak, I ask that You by Your Spirit would strengthen his flesh to obey ...

1 Corinthians 10:13 No temptation has overtaken you except such as is common to man; but God is faithful, who will not allow you to be tempted beyond what you are able, but with the temptation will also make the way of escape, that you may be able to bear it.

Prayer: I thank You Father that there is no temptation that is impossible to escape. By Your Holy Spirit, show my husband the way of escape when he is tempted to ...

James 1:12-13 Blessed is the man who endures temptation; for when he has been approved, he will receive the crown of life which the Lord has promised to those who love Him. Let no one say when he is tempted, "I am tempted by God;" for God cannot be tempted by evil, nor does He Himself tempt anyone.

Prayer: The world is full of temptations, Lord. I pray that You help my husband to endure temptation today ...

James 4:7-8 Therefore submit to God. Resist the devil and he will flee from you. Draw near to God and He will draw near to you.

Prayer: Father God, we submit our will and emotions to You today. Teach us how to resist the devil. I ask that You would draw near to my husband as he draws near to You ...

Self-Worth

Psalm 37:23-24 The steps of a good man are ordered by the Lord, and He delights in his way. Though he fall, he shall not be utterly cast down; for the Lord upholds him with His hand.

Prayer: I thank You Father that my husband is a good man. This means his steps are ordered by You Lord. I ask that You would uphold him today with Your hand …

Romans 8:16 The Spirit Himself bears witness with our spirit that we are the children of God.
    Prayer: Father I ask that You by Your Holy Spirit would bear witness with my husband's spirit that he is Your child. Give him a revelation of what it means to be Your son today …

2 Corinthians 5:17 Therefore, if anyone is in Christ, he is a new creation; old things have passed away; behold, all things have become new.
    Prayer: I thank You God that my husband is in Christ. You have made him a brand new man. His past is behind him and You are creating a new future …

Ephesians 2:8-12 For by grace you have been saved through faith, and that not of yourselves; it is the gift of God, not of works, lest anyone should boast. For we are His workmanship, created in Christ Jesus for good works, which God prepared beforehand that we should walk in them.
    Prayer: Thank You Father for Your saving grace today. My husband is Your masterpiece. You created him for good works. Reveal to him today what You have prepared for him …

1 John 4:4 You are of God, little children, and have overcome them because He who is in you in greater than he who is in the world.
    Prayer: Thank You God for making us overcomers in Christ. Greater is He who is in my husband that he who is in this world …

Fruits of the Spirit

Galatians 5:22-23 But the fruit of the Spirit is love, joy, peace, longsuffering, kindness, goodness, faithfulness, gentleness, self-control. Against such there is no law.
    Prayer: Father by Your Spirit, fill my husband to overflowing. May the fruit of the Spirit be evident in his life. I ask for more love, joy, peace, longsuffering, kindness, goodness, faithfulness, gentleness and self-control in his life …

Ephesians 4:24 and that you put on the new man which was created according to God, in true righteousness and holiness.
    Prayer: Father I ask that You teach my husband how to put on the new man today. By Your Holy Spirit, teach him how to walk in true righteousness and holiness before You God …

Ephesians 5:8-10 Walk as children of light for the Fruit of the Spirit is in all

goodness, righteousness, and truth, finding out what is acceptable to the Lord.
Prayer: Father it is our desire to walk as children of the light today. Reveal to us what is acceptable to You …

Colossians 3:14-15 But above all these things put on love, which is the bond of perfection. And let the peace of God rule in your hearts, to which also you were called in one body; and be thankful.
Prayer: Father God may your peace rule in my husband's heart today …

The human mind is a very powerful creative force in the universe. God made it this way. He gave man authority and dominion on the earth. When he told Adam to subdue the earth, it was a command to make things here on earth as you see fit. In the same way God spoke and commanded light to shine in the darkness, we have the same power to speak things into existence. Proverbs 23:7 says, *"For as he thinks in his heart, so is he."* The things that you think about with consistency eventually become your reality. A renewed mind is essential to living a victorious Christian life. What you think about over time gets down into your heart and once rooted there, becomes a part of your belief system. Luke 6:45 says, *"A good man out of the good treasure of his heart brings forth good; and an evil man out of the evil treasure of his heart brings forth evil. For out of the abundance of the heart his mouth speaks."* When you pray for your husband's soul; his mind, will and emotions to be renewed by the Spirit of God, you restore his power to change his world for the good.

There has been a lot of recent attention paid to the process whereby, thoughts become things. However, it is nothing new. Whatever you set your mind to think on is what will manifest. If you spend the majority of your time thinking that your husband is going to leave you one day, guess what, one day he'll do just that. It's counterproductive to get up early every morning and pray for your husband to be successful and do great things and then secretly believe that one day's he's going to leave home and never return. If you have any deep seated negative thoughts about yourself or your husband deal with them. Ask God to help you with your thought life. Make it your goal that all of your thoughts would be in agreement with the Word of God.

I pray that you and your husband would receive a deep revelation of who Jesus is and who you are in Him. May you be convinced of your worthiness to be called sons of God. I pray that you would understand what it means to be an heir of the Kingdom and begin to receive your inheritance. I pray that you

would both experience the full operation of the Holy Spirit in your lives as He enables the Fruit of the Spirit to operate in your lives. Amen.

SECTION FOUR

Praying for Your Husband's Body

Each of us only gets one body for this journey. It's true that we are spirit beings, but we have been given these bodies of flesh to walk around in. Praying for your husband's body is simply asking God to preserve his life. Some of our husbands have jobs that are dangerous or physically challenging. In that case, it is good to pray daily for his health and protection. If your husband is experiencing an illness or disability you will find prayers in this section that will bring healing and restore life to his body.

We don't need to obsess about our bodies but we do need to take care of them. Living with illness or caring for a spouse that is ill can be a strain on any marriage. Diseases are preventable and many are even reversible. God does not intend for any of His children to suffer and be in pain. You may have prayed for someone and they didn't get better. They may have even died. In James chapter 2:17 we are told that faith without works is dead. When it comes to having good health, it is not enough to pray, you must also do the things you know to do in order to be in good health.

You can't eat whatever you want, never exercise, smoke, or abuse drugs and then pray for God to heal you when you're on your death bed. Galatians 6:7-8 says, *"Do not be deceived, God is not mocked; for whatever a man sows, that he will also reap. For he who sows to his flesh will of the flesh reap corruption, but he who sows to the Spirit will of the Spirit reap everlasting life."* If you need a physical miracle in your body, sow seeds of health and healing. Then pray and believe God to reverse and curse the bad harvest that is due you for the seeds of sickness that you sowed in the past.

It is never too late to get started sowing good seeds. Studies have shown that when seniors begin exercising and eating right they see improvement in balance, strength and endurance. Exercise can protect against diabetes, heart disease, osteoporosis and other conditions that are considered part of the aging process. In the book of Joshua, chapter 14, Caleb tells Joshua that he is as strong today as he was 40 years ago when Moses sent them to spy out the land. Getting older doesn't necessarily mean becoming feeble and weak. God knows how to preserve your life and keep you in perfect health.

Protection

Psalm 4:8 I will both lie down in peace and sleep; for You alone, O Lord, make me dwell in safety.

Prayer: I thank You Lord, God that we are able to live in a safe place. We can lie down and sleep in peace at night because You protect those that belong to You. Father I ask for Your continued protection over my husband whenever he is away from home …

Psalm 91:1-2 He who dwells in the secret place of the Most High shall abide under the shadow of the Almighty. I will say of the Lord, "He is my refuge and my fortress; My God, in Him I will trust."

Prayer: Father I ask that You would hide my husband under Your shadow today. Be his refuge and fortress …

Psalm 91:10 No evil shall befall you, nor shall any plague come near your dwelling.

Prayer: Father You promised in Your Word that no evil will come upon us nor any plague would come near our home. I thank You Father for protecting my husband from evil today …

Isaiah 54:17 No weapon formed against you shall prosper, and every tongue which rises against you in judgment you shall condemn. This is the heritage of the servants of the Lord, and their righteousness is from Me, says the Lord.

Prayer: Thank You Father that none of the weapons that have formed against my husband will prosper. This promise is his heritage as Your servant Lord. I give You the praise everyday for protecting his life …

Ephesians 6:11-13 Put on the whole armor of God, that you may be able to stand against the wiles of the devil. For we do not wrestle against flesh and blood, but against principalities, against powers, against the rulers of the darkness of this age, against spiritual hosts of wickedness in the heavenly places. Therefore take up the whole armor of God, that you may be able to withstand in the evil day, and having done all, to stand.

Prayer: Father teach us how to fight spiritual battles today. Enable us to stand against the devil and protect us in the evil day. I pray that my husband would be completely covered and protected today ...

2 Thessalonians 3:2-3 and that we may be delivered from unreasonable and wicked men; for not all have faith. But the Lord is faithful, who will establish you and guard you from the evil one.
Prayer: Father God, I thank You that You are faithful and will protect my husband from the evil one. Deliver him from any unreasonable or wicked men he may encounter today ...

1 Peter 6:13 And who is he who will harm you if you become followers of what is good?
Prayer: Your word declares that no one can harm us if we become followers of what is good. My husband is a follower of what is good, God and I thank You for Your promise to protect, guard, and shield him from evil at all times ...

Healing

Psalm 34:19-20 Many are the afflictions of the righteous, but the Lord delivers him out of them all. He guards all his bones; not one of them is broken.
Prayer: Father I thank You for deliverance from _____. I ask that You would continue to guard every bone in my husband's body that not one of them would be broken ...

Psalm 103:2-5 Bless the Lord, O my soul, and forget not all His benefits: who forgives all your iniquities, who heals all your diseases, who redeems your life from destruction, who crowns you with loving kindness and tender mercies, who satisfies your mouth with good things, so that your youth is renewed like the eagle's.
Prayer: Today I am reminded of the benefits of worshiping You Lord. I thank You for forgiveness. I thank You that You heal all of our diseases. I ask that You redeem my husband's life from destruction. Crown him with Your loving kindness and tender mercies today. Strengthen him and renew his youth ...

Mark: 16:17-18 And these signs will follow those who believe: In My name they shall cast out demons; they will speak with new tongues; they will take up serpents; and if they drink anything deadly, it will by no means hurt them; they will lay hands on the sick, and they will recover.
Prayer: Father we believe and in the name of Jesus I cast out the demons of infirmity that have tried to attach themselves to my

husband. I thank You that Your Word says that when I lay my hands on the sick they will recover …

Romans 8:11 But if the Spirit of Him who raised Jesus from the dead dwells in you, He who raised Christ from the dead will also give life to your mortal bodies through His Spirit who dwells in you.

Prayer: I thank You God that Your Spirit dwells in my husband. May that same Spirit that raised Jesus from the dead give life to his body …

James 5:14-15 Is anyone among you sick? Let him call for the elders of the church, and let them pray over him, anointing him with oil in the name of the Lord. And the prayer of faith will save the sick, and the Lord will raise him up.

Prayer: Father I pray the prayer of faith today over my husband concerning his sickness. Lord I ask that You raise him up and make him whole again …

Well-Being

Exodus 23:25 So you shall serve the Lord your God, and He will bless your bread and your water. And I will take sickness away from the midst of you.

Prayer: We serve the Lord God. I thank You Father that You bless our food and take sickness away from us. I pray that my husband will continually live in divine health …

Psalm 27:14 Wait on the Lord; be of good courage, and He shall strengthen your heart; wait, I say, on the Lord.

Prayer: We wait on You Lord. I thank You that as my husband finds courage in waiting, You will strengthen his heart …

Proverbs 4:23 Keep your heart with all diligence, for out of it spring the issues of life.

Prayer: I thank You God for rewarding our diligence with a life that overflows …

John 8:36 Therefore if the Son makes you free, you shall be free indeed.

Prayer: Jesus You have freed my husband from the prison of sickness and pain. I thank You that he will remain free of _____ from this day forward …

3 John 1:2 Beloved, I pray that you may prosper in all things and be in health, just as your soul prospers.

Prayer: Father I come to You today and ask that my husband may prosper in all things and be in health just as his soul prospers ...

Weight Management

Isaiah 40:29 He gives power to the weak, and to those who have no might He increases strength.

Prayer: Father my husband is in need of Your power today. I ask that You would be strong when he is weak concerning the food choices he makes. Increase his strength today ...

Isaiah 55: 2-3 Why do you spend money for what is not bread, and your wages for what does not satisfy? Listen carefully to Me, and eat what is good, and let your soul delight itself in abundance. Incline your ear, and come to Me. Hear and your soul shall live; and I will make an everlasting covenant with you.

Prayer: Father I thank You for the everlasting covenant You have made with us concerning our health and well being. You have created every plant and animal for us to eat and be satisfied ...

1 Corinthians 6:12-13 All things are lawful for me, but all things are not helpful. All things are lawful for me, but I will not be brought under the power of any. Foods for the stomach and the stomach for foods, but God will destroy both it and them.

Prayer: Father God give my husband the power to resist things that may be lawful but are not helpful to his fitness goals. I pray that he would not be over powered by cravings today ...

1 Corinthians 6:19-20 Or do you not know that your body is the temple of the Holy Spirit who is in you, whom you have from God, and you are not your own? For you were bought at a price; therefore glorify God in your body and in your spirit, which are God's.

Prayer: Father God I pray that You would be glorified today in our bodies. I'm thankful that You paid the price that we may live and be in health ...

Body Image

Genesis 1:26-27 Then God said, "Let Us make man in Our image, according to Our likeness; So God created man in His own image; in the image of God He created him; male and female He created them.

Prayer: Father how awesome it is that You have created us in Your image. Your image is flawless, beautiful, and amazing. Open my husband's eyes to this fact. Let him begin to see

himself as You see him ...

1 Samuel 16:7 But the Lord said to Samuel, "Do not look at his appearance or at his physical stature, because I have refused him. For the Lord does not see as man sees; for man looks at the outward appearance, but the Lord looks at the heart."
    Prayer: I thank You Lord that You don't see as man sees. I pray that my husband would not get caught up in his outward appearance but would realize his heart is what makes him attractive ...

Psalm 138:8 The Lord will perfect that which concerns me; Your mercy O Lord, endures forever; do not forsake the works of Your hands.
    Prayer: I thank You Father, that You will perfect very area of concern and that You will never give up on the works of Your hands. Help my husband to see himself as Your work in progress. I pray he would find comfort in knowing that Your mercy towards him endures forever ...

Ecclesiastes 3:11 He has made everything beautiful in its time.
    Prayer: I thank You God that You make everything beautiful in its time. None of us gets the body we have overnight, and change can be slow, but in time You will complete the transformation. Help me to express to my husband how handsome he is to me ...

As is the case with any intercessory prayer, the person you are praying for will have to learn to pray for themselves. But until they do, God allows you to serve as an agent of change in their life. In addition to praying about the situation, also pray that your husband's faith would increase. Share relevant Scriptures with him and ask him to memorize them. In the process of memorizing the Word, he will be meditating on it. In time the Holy Spirit will give him the revelation knowledge he needs to act in faith. In Psalm 130:5, the psalmist says, "I wait for the Lord, my soul waits, and in His word do I hope." You'll need to learn to wait for the Lord. Your spirit will have no problem waiting but your soul will want to see it done, now. If you can learn to wait and place your hope in the truth of God's Word, you will receive the answers you need.

The prayer of agreement works well when it comes to asking God for healing or restored strength in the body. However, for the prayer of agreement to work, you and your husband have to believe the same thing. Before you pray together, make sure that you are on the same page concerning what you want God to do. If your husband wants to better manage his disease but you want a complete healing, it will be hard for you to pray together. In addition his underlying belief that the best he can expect is to better manage his illness will counter act your prayers for his healing. God will never violate the will of man. So find out what your husband believes and hook your faith up with his and watch God perform miracles.

Speaking daily affirmations of health and healing over yourself, your husband and children is another way to drive sickness away from you. In addition to praying and asking God about the situation. Take one of the scriptures about health or healing and make a declaration. For example, Psalm 118:17 I shall not die, but live, and declare the works of the Lord. You can get up every morning and declare that my husband will not die, but he will live and declare the works of the Lord. Continue to confess it and believe in your heart that God has not given him over to death. Even when the doctor gives you a bad report, be faithful in your declarations and stand on God's Word.

It is my prayer for you and your husband that you would both walk in divine health and healing the rest of the days of your life. I pray that you would strive to eat healthy, exercise and make regular visits to your doctor and dentist. I join my faith with yours concerning any current conditions you or your husband may have. I ask God to meet you in your place of faith concerning your health and provide deliverance from whatever ails you. I ask that He would restore any functions that were lost and strengthen any weak body parts.

SECTION FIVE

Praying for Your Husband's Finances

As much as I wish we could live in a world where money does not matter, money is a very important means of exchange. In every household, there is usually one person that is in charge of managing the finances. Regardless of which one of you manages the money in your home, praying for his livelihood will lead to increase. Money is a topic that often divides and causes strife if the two of you are not agreed about how to manage it. In addition to your prayers for your husband, you will also benefit by praying with your husband concerning money issues, investments, career changes, and tithing.

Tithing is one area of great disagreements. What do you do when one partner believes tithing is the only thing that is keeping their heads above water, and the other thinks it is the reason they are going under? The first step is to search the Scriptures for verses that describe the benefits of tithing and the curse associated with not tithing. Then sit down together and determine what you can agree to believe and then activate your faith. Start small in the beginning and expect God to bless your obedience. Diligently pray and gather your evidence in your journal as to how many times God has multiplied your tithes and offerings back to you.

The money test is one that many couples never pass. Even after years of marriage, they maintain separate bank accounts. He has his money and she has her money and the only time they discuss their finances is when it's time to pay bills. In the case where only one spouse works, the other has come to a place of trust and believe that your spouse has your best interest in mind. Both of you have to remember that you are one now and so all funds that come into the household belongs to "us" no matter who earned it. Releasing ownership of his paycheck is probably one of the hardest transitions that a husband has to make in marriage. Psalm 50 reminds us that everything in the earth belongs to God. When it comes to money, you'll both do well to remember that it's His and you are stewards of what ultimately belongs to Him.

Few of us were taught how to handle money. The little bit we know about it comes from books we've read or watching our favorite money guru on T.V. As good as that advice is, you need a financial plan that is specific to your needs. Tithing is an invitation for God to be your personal money manager. He will show you ways to make money that are perfectly aligned with your gifts and talents. He will also teach you how to make wise investments and purchases. God's economy is never in recession and He will never need to be bailed out. If you can tap into the wisdom of God for your finances, you can expect to be prosperous.

Tithing

Proverbs 3:9-10 Honor the Lord with your possessions and with the first fruits of your increase; so that your barns will be filled with plenty, and your vats overflow with new wine.

Prayer: We honor You Lord first in all things. When it comes to everything we have, we acknowledge that it is because of You that we have increased. My husband and I will continue to honor You with our tithe and believe You to fill our lives with plenty and cause it to overflow ...

Malachi 3:8 Will a man rob God? Yet you have robbed Me! But you say, In what way have we robbed You? In tithes and offerings.

Prayer: Father we have determined that we will not rob You. We will be faithful to freely give our tithes and offerings to our local church. At times my husband's faith to tithe needs to be increased. I ask that You would reveal to him all the blessings of the tithe ...

Malachi 3:10 Bring all the tithes into the storehouse, that there may be food in My house, and try Me now in this, says the Lord of hosts, If I will not open for you the windows of heaven and pour out for you such blessing that there will not be room enough to receive it.

Prayer: Father God I thank You for open windows of blessings over our household because of our tithes. Give us wisdom concerning what to do with the overflow that You have promised in Your Word ...

Career Advancement/Promotion

Psalm 37:34 Wait on the Lord, and keep His way, and He will exalt you to inherit the land.

Prayer: I thank You Lord that Your word promises to exalt us if we would wait on You and keep Your ways. Comfort my husband's heart today. Remind him of this promise today Lord …

Psalm 75:6-7 For exaltation comes neither from the east nor from the west nor from the south. But God is the Judge: He puts down one and exalts another.

Prayer: I thank You Lord that promotion comes from Your hand. I ask that You would be the judge concerning my husband's work. Cause him to be noticed by his superiors and considered for pay raises and increase …

Luke 12:32 Do not fear, little flock, for it is your Father's good pleasure to give you the kingdom.

Prayer: Father, it is Your desire to give us the kingdom. So we will not fear or be too concerned about the trivial things in this world. I believe that part of giving us the kingdom includes providing a means of making a good living …

Luke 16:10 He who is faithful in what is least is faithful also in much; and he who is unjust in what is least is unjust also in much.

Prayer: I thank You Father that as my husband continues to be faithful where he is, you will give him more responsibility and rank on his job. I pray that he would not become frustrated with the little he does now because his little part is valuable to the whole …

Colossians 3:23-24 And whatever you do, do it heartily, as to the Lord and not to men, knowing that from the Lord you will receive the reward of the inheritance; for you serve the Lord Christ.

Prayer: I ask that You would remind my husband that his reward will come from You and not his boss …

James 1:17 Every good gift and every perfect gift is from above, and comes down from the Father of lights, with whom there is no variation or shadow of turning.

Prayer: I thank You God that every good and perfect gift comes from You. My husband's current job has been a blessing to our family. Any future promotion or new jobs will be gifts from You as well …

1 Peter 5:5-7 God resists the proud, but gives grace to the humble. Therefore humble yourselves under the mighty hand of God that He may exalt you in due time, casting all your care upon Him, for He cares for you.

Prayer: **Father I thank You for giving grace to the humble. I ask that You daily remind my husband to walk in humility. I believe in due time you will exalt him and lift him up ...**

Wisdom on how to maneuver office politics

Psalm 23:4-5 Yea, though I walk through the valley of the shadow of death, I will fear no evil; for You are with me; Your rod and Your staff, they comfort me. You prepare a table before me in the presence of my enemies; You anoint my head with oil; my cup runs over.

Prayer: **Father I ask that You would guide and comfort my husband today as he deals with politics and bureaucracy in the workplace. I pray that You would prepare a place of great provision for him even in the presence of people who would try to hinder his progress ...**

Proverbs 3:3-4 Let not mercy and truth forsake you; bind them around your neck, write them on a tablet for your heart, and so find favor and high esteem in the sight of God and man.

Prayer: **Father I pray that my husband would find favor and high esteem in Your sight. May he also find favor and high esteem with his co-workers ...**

Romans 11:29 For the gifts and the callings of God are irrevocable.

Prayer: **I thank You God that Your gifts and callings are irrevocable. The natural abilities that You have blessed with my husband with can not be taken from him. I ask today that You would cause his gift to make room for him in his workplace ...**

1 Corinthians 14:40 Let all things be done decently and in order.

Prayer: **Father I know that You are a God of order and not of chaos. I pray that everything in my husband's office would be done decently and in order as unto You God ...**

Philippians 2:3-4 Let nothing be done through selfish ambition or conceit, but in lowliness of mind let each esteem others better than himself. Let each of you look not only for his own interests, but also for the interest of others.

Prayer: **Father God, my husband is a team player. He is not motivated by selfish ambition or conceit. He looks out for the interest of the others on his team and I ask that You would bless** the entire company because of him …

Wisdom for the Entrepreneur

Deuteronomy 8:18 And you shall remember the Lord your God, for it is He who gives you power to get wealth, that He may establish His covenant which He swore to your fathers, as it is this day.

Prayer: Lord God, I ask that You would give my husband the power to get wealth today. Establish Your covenant thorough him and his business …

Psalm 127:1-6 Unless the Lord builds the house, they labor in vain who build it.

Prayer: I thank You Lord that You are building our business. I pray that my husband's labor would never be in vain …

Proverbs 10:22 The blessings of the Lord makes one rich, and He adds no sorrow with it.

Prayer: I thank You Father that Your blessings will make my husband rich. When Your blessings are manifested in our lives, there will be no sorrow with it, and he can make good use of the money for helping needy people, expanding the Kingdom of God, …

Proverbs 13:11 Wealth gained by dishonesty will be diminished but he who gathers by labor will increase.

Prayer: My husband is one who gains wealth by honest means and hard work. Father I ask you to provide the increase in his business. I ask for new clients, bigger deals, and stability in the Name of Jesus …

Proverbs 28:20 A faithful man will abound with blessings, but he who hastens to be rich will not go unpunished.

Prayer: I thank You Father for giving me a faithful man. I pray that he would abound with blessings, according to Your Word. May he always do what's right and not cut corners in an attempt to get rich quick …

Hebrews 13:5 Let your conduct be without covetousness; be content with such things as you have. For He Himself has said, "I will never leave you nor forsake you."

Prayer: Father I pray that You will remind my husband daily that You are his business partner and that You will never leave him. Teach him to be content with the things he has and not become envious of his competitors …

1Timothy 6:10 For the love of money is the root of all kinds of evil, for which some have strayed from the faith in their greediness, and pierced themselves through with many sorrows.

Prayer: **Father I ask that You by Your Spirit would guard my husband's heart from greed. I pray that he would never stray from the faith in pursuit of money ...**

1 Timothy 6:17 Command those who are rich in this present age not to be haughty, nor to trust in uncertain riches but in the living God, who gives us richly all things to enjoy.

Prayer: **Father God, when the blessing comes we will continue to trust in You and give You thanks for all the things You have given us to enjoy ...**

James 5:12 But above all, my brethren, do not swear, either by heaven or by earth or with any other oath. But let your Yes be Yes, and your No, No, lest you fall into judgment.

Prayer: **Father I thank You that You have made my husband to be a man of his word. I pray that no matter what the circumstance, his Yes will always be Yes and his No will always be No ...**

Budgeting

Proverbs 22:26-27 Do not be one of those who shakes hands in a pledge, one of those who is surety for debts; if you have nothing with which to pay, why should he take away your bed from under you?

Pray: **Father I ask that You would instruct my husband on how to use debt. Teach him how to budget wisely and not overextend himself with more obligations than he can pay each month ...**

Luke 14:28 For which of you, intending to build a tower, does not sit down first and count the cost, whether he has enough to finish it.

Prayer: **Teach us how to count the cost God in every money decision we make. Impress upon my husband's heart the importance of budgeting. Help him to see that it is not a restriction on spending but a plan for spending ...**

Luke 16:11 Therefore if you have not been faithful in the unrighteous mammon, who will commit to your trust the true riches?

Prayer: **Father we desire to become good stewards of the resources You have given us. My husband is faithful with the** money he has now and I pray that You will see fit to trust him with true riches ...

2 Corinthians 9:8 And God is able to make all grace abound toward you, that you, always having all sufficiency in all things, may have an abundance for every good work.

Prayer: God I thank You for grace that abounds toward us that as we budget we find that we always have what we need. My husband and I are never limited but have an abundance for every good work that needs to be done, serving our community, and be Your witness to people ...

Investments

Proverbs 6:6-11 Go to the ant, you sluggard! Consider her ways and be wise, which having no captain, overseer or ruler, provides her supplies in the summer, and gathers her food in the harvest. How long will you slumber, o sluggard? When will you rise from your sleep? A little sleep, a little slumber, a little folding of the hands to sleep – so shall your poverty come on you like a prowler, and your need like an armed man.

Prayer: Father we know that the time to save for the future is now. I thank You that my husband is wise and alert to the need for wise investments ...

Proverbs 13:22 A good man leaves an inheritance to his children's children, but the wealth of the sinner is stored up for the righteous.

Prayer: I thank You Father that my husband is a good man. I ask that You would guide us to the right investments so that we may leave an inheritance to our grandchildren ...

Haggai 1:6 You have sown much, and bring in little; you eat, but do not have enough; you drink, but you are not filled with drink; you clothe yourselves, but no one is warm; and he who earns wages, earns wages to put into a bag with holes.

Prayer: Father God we refuse to live hand to mouth. I ask in the Name of Jesus that You would lead my husband in such a way that he would avoid the curse of poverty. Make his labor to be fruitful and bring a return on all that has been sown ...

Matthew 6:19 Do not lay up for yourselves treasures on earth, where moth and rust destroy and where thieves break in and steal; but lay up for yourselves in heaven, where neither moth nor rust destroys and where thieves do not break in a steal. For where your treasure is, there your heart will be also.

Prayer: Even though we have some savings here on earth, Father we are also mindful that our hearts must remain pure towards You. We know that what we have here can be stolen or destroyed …

Balance between Work and Home

Genesis 2:2-3 And on the seventh day God ended His work which He had done, and He rested on the seventh day from all His work which He had done. Then God blessed the seventh day and sanctified it, because in it He rested from all His work which God had created and made.

Prayer: Father I ask You to teach my husband how to rest. Just as you have sanctified a day specifically for rest, I pray that my husband would heed Your example …

Exodus 20:9 Six days you shall labor and do all your work.

Prayer: Father You have given us six days in order to do work and take care of our business. I pray that my husband would find balance in this, that he would strive to get work done at work and choose to rest and play when he is home …

Ecclesiastes 3: 9-10; 12-13 What profit has the worker from that in which he labors? I have seen the God-given task with which the sons of men are to be occupied. I know that nothing is better for them than to rejoice, and to do good in their lives, and also that every man should eat and drink and enjoy the good of all his labor – it is the gift of God.

Prayer: Father teach my husband how to relax and enjoy the fruits of his labor. I thank You for this gift that You give to man …

Time Management

Psalm 90:12 So teach us to number our days, that we may gain a heart of wisdom.

Prayer: Father I acknowledge that the days left on earth are short. Teach us how to make the most of every minute we have. Show my husband how to use his time wisely …

Ephesians 5:15-16 See then that you walk circumspectly, not as fools but as wise, redeeming the time, because the days are evil.

Prayer: Father I ask that You would teach my husband how to redeem the time he has lost on things that did not profit …

Prosperity is a topic that many in the church don't know if they should be for it or against it. The reality is that most of us can use a little more money. When you are in prayer asking for wisdom on how to invest what you have, also ask God about the purpose for amassing large quantities of money. Ask Him to show you the people you can help and what Kingdom projects you can fund if there were excess funds in your bank account. Remember money is not evil. However, if our intentions for obtaining money are evil or selfish God won't release it to us.

God's covenant to man includes prosperity. We read in 2 Chronicles 1:10-12 how King Solomon asked God to give him wisdom and knowledge that he may judge the people of God. In verse 11 God said to Solomon, "Because this was in your heart, and you have not asked riches or wealth or honor or the life of your enemies, nor have you asked long life – but have asked wisdom and knowledge for yourself, that you may judge My people over whom I have made you king – wisdom and knowledge are granted to you; and I will give you riches and wealth and honor, such as none of the kings have had who were before you, nor shall any after you have the like."

Although no man was as blessed as Solomon there are many rich men of the Bible. They walked close to God in humble obedience and God rewarded them with riches, honor and long life. In addition He kept His covenant with their family for generations. You can rest assured that once you receive God's wisdom and knowledge concerning your finances that your children's children will reap the benefits.

It is my prayer that you and your husband would have the mind of Christ concerning your finances. I pray that you would make wise decisions concerning tithing, budgeting, and investing. May you both be blessed with a means of making money that satisfies your soul and allows you to be the best of who God created you to be everyday.

SECTION SIX

Praying for Your Husband's Heart

You've already won your husband's heart. But you'll have to work to maintain the bond and affection you feel for one another. Who says the honeymoon has to ever end? Why can't you be as in love today as you were the day you said, "I do"? In fact, you should be more in love today than ever because of the things you have gone through together. For some this section will be about maintaining, for others it will be about reclaiming intimacy that was lost.

Companionship, trust and sexual expression are crucial parts of a marriage relationship. Complete surrender is required. If you have trust issues, there will be trouble in paradise. Boundaries also need to be firmly established in marriage. You must maintain key relationships with family and friends in order to not become isolated. Isolation is the beginning of the end for most marriages. Most importantly, you'll need to maintain your fellowship with God the Father. At times, He may be the only person you can run to. Your husband won't be able to meet your every need. It's actually unrealistic to expect that he will. There will be some things that only God can do in and through you.

I doubt that a wife can ever truly understand the pressure that husbands feel concerning providing for their families. Many of them work and quietly carry the weight of the world on their shoulders. It may seem to you that he has no time or room for you and the children. When in reality, you and the children have consumed him to the point where he has worn himself out serving you. A man's identity and self-esteem is tied up in how well he takes care of his family. If you have struggled financially, he may carry a sin of shame or feel that he has let you down. This shame can manifest itself as anger, resentment or a lack of desire. He'll want to pull away because he feels less than adequate in your presence. That is when you will have to make the first move and reassure him of your continued devotion and unfailing love for him. God loves us with an everlasting, unconditional love. This is the same kind of love; you'll need to show your husband during times of uncertainty.

Intimacy

Genesis 2:24 Therefore a man shall leave his father and mother and be joined to his wife, and they shall become one flesh.

Prayer: Father it is my desire that we would become one flesh according to Your word. I thank You for the special times my husband and I have had together and for all the memories we have built together ...

Psalm 133:1 Behold, how good and how pleasant it is for brethren to dwell together in unity!

Prayer: Father I thank You for the blessing that You give us when we dwell together in unity ...

Proverbs 5:18-19 Let your fountain be blessed, and rejoice with the wife of your youth. As a loving deer and a graceful doe, let her breast satisfy you at all times; and always be enraptured with her love.

Prayer: Lord God, I ask that you give me the grace to be the type of wife that my husband can rejoice with. I desire to bless him always and be a safe place for him to rest his head when he is weary ...

Song of Solomon 2:16 My beloved is mine, and I am his.

Prayer: Father it is my desire to develop more intimacy with my husband. I pray for opportunities to show him in big ways and small ways that I am his and he is mine ...

1 Corinthians 7:2-5 Nevertheless, because of sexual immorality, let each man have his own wife, and let each woman have her own husband. Let the husband rend to his wife the affection due her, and likewise also wife to her husband. The wife does not have authority over her own body, but the husband does. And likewise the husband does not have authority over his own body, but the wife does. Do not deprive on another except with consent for a time that you may give yourselves to fasting and prayer; and come together again so that Satan does not tempt you because of your lack of self-control.

Prayer: Father I thank You for sanctifying marriage. I thank You for intimacy in marriage that is like no other relationship on earth ...

Sexuality

Song of Solomon 1:16 Behold, you are handsome, my beloved! Yes, pleasant! Also our bed is green.

Prayer: Lord God I thank You for my beloved husband. I pray that our desire for one another would never fade or become dull …

Galatians 5:16-17 I say then: Walk in the Spirit, and you shall not fulfill the lust of the flesh. For the flesh lust against the Spirit, and the Spirit against the flesh; and these are contrary to one another, so that you do not do the things that you wish.

Prayer: Father I pray that my husband would walk continually in the Spirit so that he would not fulfill the lust of his flesh. I pray that by your Holy Spirit he would have the power to withstand lust …

Galatians 5:24 And those who are Christ's have crucified the flesh with its passions and desires.

Prayer: Thank You God for killing the old desires of the flesh when we came to Christ. Thank You for replacing lust with a mature love and respect. Thank You for purifying our passions and desires for one another …

1 Thessalonians 4:3-5 For this is the will of God, your sanctification: that you should abstain from sexual immorality; that each of you should know how to possess his own vessel in sanctification and honor, not in passion of lust, like the Gentiles who do not know God.

Prayer: Father God I ask that You would continue to sanctify us through our marriage union. Teach us to possess our bodies and honor them by not seeking satisfaction outside of our union …

Hebrews 13:4 Marriage is honorable among all, and the bed undefiled; but fornicators and adulterers God will judge.

Prayer: Father you have made marriage an honorable institution. I thank You for the freedom You have given us to express our sexual desires with one another and to please one another without fear or shame …

Love

Proverbs 10:12 Hatred stirs up strife, but love covers all sins.

Prayer: I thank You God that love covers a multitude of sins.

Teach us how to walk in love with one another that we may never live in hatred and strife ...

Malachi 2:14-16 Yet you say, "For what reason?" Because the Lord has been witness between you and the wife of your youth, with whom you have dealt treacherously; Yet she is your companion and Your wife by covenant. But did He not make them one, Having a remnant of the Spirit? And why one? He seeks godly offspring. Therefore take heed to your spirit, and let none deal treacherously with the wife of his youth. For the Lord God of Israel says that He hates divorce.

Prayer: Lord God, I recognize that Your Word says that You hate divorce. When we married, my husband and I entered into a covenant relationship. Father I ask that You would be the mediator between us ...

John 15:12-13 This is My commandment, that you love one another as I have loved you. Greater love has no one than this, than to lay down one's life for his friends.

Prayer: Lord teach us to love one another as You have loved us. Help us to display this selfless love at all times. Father, teach us to lay down our lives for one another ...

1 Corinthians 13:1-3 Though I speak with tongues of men and of angels, but have not love, I have become a sounding brass or a clanging cymbal. And though I have the gift of prophecy, and understand mysteries and all knowledge, and though I have all faith, so that I could remove mountains, but have not love, I am nothing. And though I bestow all my goods to feed the poor, and though I give my body to be burned, but have not love, it profits me nothing.

Prayer: Father we endeavor to make love the principle thing in our marriage. Teach us how to love as You love, God; to always give our best to one another ...

Galatians 5:14-15 For all the law is fulfilled in one word, even this: "You shall love your neighbor as yourself." But if you bite and devour one another, beware lest you be consumed by one another!

Prayer: Father I pray that we would grow more in love with one another each day and that we would love one another as we love ourselves. May we never do or say anything that would destroy the other ...

Ephesians 5:25;28 Husbands, love your wives, just as Christ also loved the church and gave Himself for her, so husbands ought to love their own wives as their own bodies; he who loves his wife loves himself.

Prayer: I thank You God for giving me a husband who loves me just as Christ loved the church. He has been willing to give up things he has wanted to provide for me and the family. I ask

that You would bless him and keep him ...

Colossians 3:19 Husbands love your wives and do not be bitter toward them.
    Prayer: In the name of Jesus, I bind any bitterness that would try to attach itself to my husband. May he always love me and seek my good as You have commanded him in Your Word God ...

1 Peter 3:7 Husbands, likewise, dwell with them with understanding, giving honor to the wife, as the weaker vessel, and as being heirs together of the grace of life, that your prayers may not be hindered.
    Prayer: Father by Your Spirit teach my husband how to dwell with me in understanding. I ask that he would always find ways to honor me. I thank You Father for making us heirs together of the grace of life ...

Trust

Psalm 118:8 It is better to trust the Lord than to put confidence in man.
    Prayer: Father teach me to trust You Lord. I pray that my confidence would not be solely in my husband alone but that I can trust the God that is in him ...

Proverbs 3:5-6 Trust in the Lord with all your heart, and lean not on your own understanding; in all of your ways acknowledge Him, and He shall direct your paths.
    Prayer: Father I trust in You with all of my heart and I will not trust in my own understanding of situations. We acknowledge You Father as the head of our lives and the glue that holds our marriage together. Lead, guide and direct us God into a more perfect trust ...

Isaiah 26:3 You will keep him in perfect peace, whose mind is stayed on You, because he trusts in You.
    Prayer: Father thank You for giving perfect peace when we keep our minds focused on You. May we choose to trust the God in one another and always think the best of each other ...

    I think the best piece of advice on marriage is found in Ephesians 4:26-27, "Be angry, and do not sin," do not let the sun go down on your wrath, nor give place to the devil. The enemy of your soul would love nothing more than to destroy your marriage. The first thing Satan did in the earth was to drive a wedge between Adam and Eve. He deceived Eve and got her to doubt God's Word. She got Adam to join her in her rebellion. And with one bite of the forbidden fruit, Satan was able to isolate them from God; destroy the intimacy between Adam and Eve; and cause them not to trust one another. Daily prayer in this area will keep you in right relationship with God. This will enable you to maintain the intimacy, trust, and love you have with your husband. Prayer and communion with the Holy Spirit will leave no room for the devil to creep into your marriage.

The last piece of advice I'd like to share with you is found in 1 Peter 5:8-9, Be sober, be vigilant; because your adversary the devil walks about like a roaring lion, seeking whom he may devour. Resist him, steadfast in the faith, knowing that the same sufferings are experienced by your brotherhood in the world. You can't afford to live your life on auto pilot. The minute you get caught just going through the motions in your marriage, the devil will devour you. You must be awake, vigilant, and remain in faith in order to resist the devil and watch him flee. Also know that you are not alone, because every marriage is under attack.

Proverbs 14:1 The wise woman builds her house, but the foolish pulls it down with her hands. When a husband is found to be unfaithful, the wife is quick to blame the husband, or the mistress. But I would encourage you to make sure that you were not like the foolish woman in Proverbs 14 who has pulled your house down with your own hands. We are not to be arrogant and believe that no other woman could win our husband's affections. However, we must make sure that we have not behaved in ways that would drive our husband into the arms of another.

A successful marriage glorifies God. A marriage that lasts, displays God's love for the world to see. I believe that when the divorce rate among Christians decreases, we will see an increase in the new births. Many of the problems we face in society are a result of failed families. When marriage works, children are raised in a loving environment and grow up to be productive members of society. Marriage is an important ministry that many are ill prepared for. Few really understand what is at stake.

I pray that God would give you and your husband a vision for your marriage. That He would reveal to you His heart concerning marriage. That He would share with you the purpose for which he joined you and your husband together. I pray that your love for one another would never fail, but rather grow deeper every day. In the name of Jesus, Amen.

SECTION SEVEN

Praying for Your Husband's Legacy

Each of us has been given a specific assignment here on earth, but regardless of that assignment, we are all commanded to leave a legacy. Genesis 1:28 tells us to be fruitful and to multiply and replenish the earth. God has always been concerned about future generations. God repeatedly talked to Abraham about his seed, or his descendants being blessed. The laws of seed time and harvest found throughout the Bible can be applied to any and every thing. When it comes to making a mark and leaving a legacy, the seeds sown today will produce a harvest that can be maintained for generations.

When someone amasses huge sums of money during their lifetime, they usually set up a trust fund or an endowment to make sure that their money continues to support their favorite causes after they die. The same thing can be done in the spirit. We should all leave a spiritual legacy for those that come after us. This legacy is not only for our children and grandchildren but can also be for our communities. The prayers in this section are geared toward husbands that have a leadership role either in the local church or community. However, I believe we all have something to contribute and these prayers can be prayed for anyone who wants to impact their world in some way.

It's never too soon to begin thinking about the type of legacy you want to leave. The decisions you make today will shape your tomorrow and either add or detract from your legacy. We should all attempt to live a life that is above reproach. This doesn't mean we will be perfect or never make mistakes. But it does mean we will do our best to walk in integrity and be as authentic as we can with the people God has given us to lead or influence. People want to know that you are real. That if they prick you, you will bleed. Even Jesus told the rich young ruler in Mark 10: 18 "Why do you call Me good? No one is good but

One, that is, God." And it will take God by the power of the Holy Spirit working in you and your husband to leave a legacy that brings honor and glory to Him.

Leadership

1 Corinthians 11:3 But I want you to know that the head of every man is Christ, the head of woman is man, and the head of Christ is God.

Prayer: Thank You Father for establishing Your order in the earth. According to Your Word, You are the supreme leader over all, followed by Christ who is the leader of every man. You have given my husband the responsibility of being leader of me and our children. Help him to daily walk in this leadership …

Ephesians 5:23 For the husband is head of the wife, as also Christ is head of the church; and He is the Savior of the body.

Prayer: I ask Father that You would teach my husband how to lead in a Christ like fashion. I pray that he would take on the role of servant leader and lead with compassion and love …

Colossians 3:17 And whatever you do in word or deed, do all in the name of the Lord Jesus, giving thanks unto God the Father through Him.

Prayer: I pray that my husband would do everything in the Name of the Lord Jesus. Every word, every deed done in an attitude of worship to You Father God …

Hebrews 13:17 Obey those who rule over you, and be submissive, for they watch out for your souls, as those who must give account. Let them do so with joy and not with grief, for that would be unprofitable for you.

Prayer: Father God I submit my heart to my husband as he is one who rules over me and watches for my soul. I ask that You would give him joy in this responsibility …

1 Timothy 5:17 Let the elders who rule well be counted worthy of a double honor, especially those who labor in the word and doctrine.

Prayer: Father God my husband is an elder and he rules well. I ask that you would count him worthy to receive double honor for his labor in the word and doctrine …

Faithfulness

Deuteronomy 7:9 Therefore know that the Lord your God, He is God, the faithful God who keep covenant and mercy for a thousand generations with those who love Him and keep His commandments.

Prayer: Lord God You are faithful and I love You. I thank You for the covenant You have made with us, giving mercy for a thousand generations. I thank You for giving me a husband who is faithful as You are faithful, who loves you and endeavors to keep Your commandments ...

1 Samuel 26:23 May the Lord repay every man for his righteousness and his faithfulness.
Prayer: Father I ask that You would repay my husband for his righteousness and his faithfulness to Your Word ...

Matthew 5:28 But I say unto you that whoever looks at a woman to lust for her has already committed adultery with her in his heart.
Prayer: Father I pray that You would place a guard over my husbands eyes and his heart that he may not lust for another woman. I pray that he would never become susceptible to the advances of another woman ...

1 Corinthians 4:2 Moreover it is required in stewards that one be found faithful.
Prayer: You have required that Your stewards be faithful. I thank You that my husband has been a faithful steward of everything You have given him ...

Fatherhood

Psalm 127:3-5 Behold children are a heritage from the Lord, the fruit of the womb is a reward. Like arrows in the hand of a warrior, so are the children of one's youth. Happy is the man who has is quiver full of them.
Prayer: I thank You God that our children were given to us as a reward. I pray that my husband would be happy and blessed because of our many children ...

Proverbs 13:24 He who spares his rod hates his son, but he who loves him disciplines him promptly.
Prayer: Father I pray that my husband would always promptly discipline our children so that they will know they are loved and cared for ...

Proverbs 20:7 The righteous man walks in his integrity; his children are blessed after him.
Prayer: I thank You God that my husband is a righteous man who walks in integrity. I pray that our children will follow his

example and be blessed ...

Proverbs 22:6 Train up a child in the way he should go, and when he is old he will not depart from it.
    Prayer: We stand on Your promise God, that if we train our children in righteousness they will not depart from what we teach them. I pray that no matter how old they get, they will always be able to come to us in times of uncertainty. Even more that they would always remember what we have taught them about You ...

Isaiah 54:13 All your children shall be taught by the Lord, and great shall be the peace of your children.
    Prayer: Father God my husband is a godly example to our children, teaching them to fear and love You Lord. I thank You for the great peace upon our children and our household ...

Colossians 3:21 Fathers, do not provoke your children, lest they become discouraged.
    Prayer: My husband is careful not to provoke our children but rather encourages them to do their best. Father, continue to strengthen the bond between my husband and our children ...

Contributions to Society

John 13:34-35 A new commandment I give to you, that you love one another; as I have loved you, that you also love one another. By this all will know that you are My disciples, if you have love for one another.
    Prayer: Father I pray that my husband would leave a legacy of love. Let it be said of him that he is Your disciple because of the love he has for his fellow man ...

Acts 6:4 But we will give ourselves continually to prayer and to the ministry of the word.
    Prayer: Father God I thank You that my husband is one who gives himself to prayer continually and gives himself completely to the ministry of Your Word ...

Romans 12:9-13 Let love be without hypocrisy. Abhor what is evil. Cling to what is good. Be kindly affectionate to one another with brotherly love, in honor giving preference to one another; not lagging in diligence, fervent in spirit, serving the Lord; rejoicing in hope, patient in tribulation, continuing steadfastly in prayer; distributing to the needs of the saints, given to hospitality.
    Prayer: Father I pray that my husband would always cling to what is good and never lack diligence when it comes to serving You. I pray that he would be patient in tribulations and always

pray concerning the needs of others ...

Colossians 1:10 That you may walk worthy of the Lord, fully pleasing Him, being fruitful in every good work and increasing in the knowledge of God.
    Prayer: Father I pray that my husband would be found pleasing in your sight today, that he would be fruitful in every good work and increase in the knowledge of You ...

1 Thessalonians 5:23-24 Now may the God of peace Himself sanctify you completely; and may your whole spirit, soul and body be preserved blameless at the coming of our Lord Jesus Christ. He who calls you is faithful, who also will do it.
    Prayer: Father I judge You as faithful to completely sanctify my husband's whole spirit, soul and body. I ask that he would be found blameless at the returning of Your son Jesus Christ ...

2 Thessalonians 1:11-12 Therefore we also pray always for you that our God would count you worthy for this calling, and fulfill all the good pleasure of His goodness and the work of faith with power, that the name of the Lord Jesus Christ may be glorified in you, and you in Him, according to the grace of our God and the Lord Jesus Christ.
    Prayer: Father I pray that You would always count my husband worthy of the calling You have placed upon his life. May the Lord Jesus Christ be glorified in his life and through his legacy ...

Whether your husband is a deacon, head usher, preacher, teacher, policeman, or mechanic, God can use him in the Kingdom. Whatever his place of influence, he can be used to shine the light of the Gospel. If your husband has been called to a role of leadership, always remember that he is still a man. More importantly, he is your man, so make sure you take care of him. When he's out with the people he is serving, step back and let him do his thing. Support him through your prayers and any assistance he may ask of you. But when he is home, allow him to take off the mask and be the real, fallible, human being that he is.

There is a tendency to put our role models on a pedestal and believe that they are perfect in every way. You, as his wife must remember that he is not perfect. There will be times when he'll need your forgiveness and mercy. Your diligent prayers in this area can be the difference between your husband having a good legacy or a legacy that is tarnished. Living with a public person is not easy and it requires even more grace from you as his wife, but God will give you the grace. He will give you the wisdom as to how to keep some things private and just between the two of you. There is a delicate balance between how much of yourselves you give away to the ministry and how much you keep.

Behind every great man is a great woman. You are more than just the wife of [insert your husband's name], but you are the driving force behind his greatness. He is the man that he is because of your love, your prayers, and your encouragement. He may get all of the public applause but God is very pleased with a wife who uses her live in service to her husband. For those of you who have been given a gift of leadership it will be tempting to compete with your husband, but avoid it at all cost. Ephesians 4:3-6 says, "Endeavoring to keep the unity of the Spirit in the bond of peace. There is only one body and one Spirit, just as you were called in one hope of your calling; one Lord, one faith, one baptism; one God and Father of all, who is above all, and through all, and in you all." The two of you are on the same team and there is only one leader. So you must endeavor to keep the unity of the Spirit in the bond of peace in your marriage. God will give you a place to shine that doesn't undermine your husband's authority, if you faithfully defer to your husband and allow God to direct you.

I pray that God would give you the grace to live with a man who has been called to public leadership. May You receive the blessing that comes with sharing him with the world. I pray that you would be your husband's anchor and a safe harbor for him when he comes home. I ask God to increase his influence and give him great favor. Amen.

CONCLUSION

In conclusion, I'd like to congratulate you on taking the first steps toward building a strong foundation for your marriage. To those who have been married for years, I applaud you for taking the steps to ensure continued longevity. Like anything else worth having, marriage is hard work. The fact that two very different people can get married and in time become one has got to be one of the greatest mysteries. Lucky for us, God will reveal the mystery to us through prayer. Mark 4:11 tell us that we are to know the mystery of the kingdom of God. We are not to remain ignorant of God's ways. He wants you to know how marriage works. More specifically, he want to teach you how to make your marriage work.

When a couple goes through pre-marital counseling, the first concept that is often presented is the idea of a Christ centered marriage. They are admonished to keep God first and everything else will be alright. What is often missing from these discussions is the how. How do you make sure that God is a partner in your marriage? The one tried and true way I know to keep God first and Christ in the center of whatever it is I'm doing is to pray. When you pray and exercise your faith daily, amazing things will begin to happen. Where there was strife, there will be peace. Where there was sadness, there will be joy. Even a marriage that seems to be doomed to fail can be saved through the power of prayer. No situation is beyond hope where the prayer of faith is concerned. If you desire to be reconciled with your mate, your marriage can be restored by the power of prayer.

There is no more powerful force on earth than a husband and wife who have learned to work together. Ecclesiastes 4:9-12 says, "Two are better than one, because they have a good reward for their labor. For it they fall, one will lift up his companion. But woe to him who is alone when he falls, for he has no one to help him up. Again, if two lie down together, they will keep warm; but how can one be warm alone? Though one may be overpowered by another, two can withstand him. And a threefold cord is not quickly broken." Before you got married it was you and the God. After you got married it is you, God and your husband. This I believe is the threefold cord that this scripture is talking about. There is so much power in unity. It pleases the Father and He will command a blessing over a couple that continually walks in unity.

Remember, a house divided can not stand. In Matthew 12:25, Jesus told the Pharisees that, "Every kingdom divided against itself is brought to desolation, and every city or house divided against itself will not stand." Prayer for your husband and with your husband is the glue that binds the two of you together. Constant prayer enables the two of you to present a united front against the enemy. If you search the scriptures you will find that God is as god of symmetry. He likes doing things in groups of two. The number two represents balance, harmony, union and division. The animals went into the ark in groups of two. The ark of the covenant was covered by two cherubim. The law given to Moses was written on two tablets. In most of the parables of Jesus, the number 2 features prominently. There was a man with two sons, a woman give two mites, the disciples were sent out in twos and even Jesus was crucified between two thieves. Begin to tap into the power of two when you come into agreement with your husband concerning the will of God for your marriage.

The role of wife can sometimes be accompanied by hardship and sorrow. However, God never intended for marriage to be a prison sentence. His intention from the beginning was for Adam and Eve to live together in harmony, in a place where they lacked nothing. As we know, the sin of disobedience caused them to be evicted from the garden and they were made to live under a curse. The good news of the Gospel for your marriage is this: Jesus came to remove the curse and restore all that was lost in the garden. Galatians 3:13 says, Christ has redeemed us from the curse of the law, having become a curse for us (for it is written, "Cursed is everyone who hangs on a tree.") Because we are children of God, our marriages should be full of joy, peace, love, tenderness and forgiveness. Every husband should strive to love his wife as Christ loved the church and every wife submitting to her husband as unto the Lord. You can't have one side without the other because the husband's love makes the wife's submission easier. And as you have probably discovered, the wife's submission causes her husband's love for her to grow.

When you have a husband that is submitted to God and humbly leads his family, and a wife who joyfully submits to her husband, marriage becomes all that God intended it to be. The man has a purpose and finds fulfillment and the woman and children are protected and taken care of. Strong, healthy families cause the society to flourish and we get to experience a little bit of heaven here on earth. Put all of the cynicism you've heard about marriage out of your mind and renew your mind in the Word of God. Marriage is one of the things that God has given us to enjoy. Never see it as drudgery or even a duty, but rather a pleasure. Serving your husband is not something you "have to" but something you "get to" do. It really is a matter of perspective and attitude, both of which will improve as you pray for your husband.

I'll leave you with this final thought, James 5:16 says, "The effective, fervent prayer of a righteous man avails much." The Amplified Bible put it this way, The earnest (heartfelt, continued) prayer of a righteous man makes tremendous power available [dynamic in its working]. At times we think of prayer as a passive thing. But this verse tells us there is nothing passive about prayer. In fact, prayer actually gets things done. It makes tremendous power available that is dynamic in its working. Be assured that your earnest continual prayer for your husband will changes things in ways you can't even imagine now. Issues that you've struggled with for years will become non-issues once you begin to pray. As you pray the Word of God, remnants of the curse that were in operation in your life will be cancelled and made of no affect.

Praying for your husband everyday is the best investment you can make into your marriage. The return on your investment of prayer is almost immediate and will pay big dividends with each passing year. God will not only bless your marriage but he will use you to bless other married couples. You can share with other married women how much praying for your husband has changed your life and improved your marriage. It is my hearts desire that every wife would learn to pray for her husband and that more husbands and wives would pray together. If you were blessed and greatly helped by this book, I ask that you would pay it forward by sharing this book with all the women in your life.

I pray that is book would encourage many wives to pray for their husbands every day. I pray that the prayers of the wives would build their husbands up, and make their hearts tender toward them. I ask that God would show up big on behalf of every woman who give herself to prayer for her husband and children. Father I know You heart's desire is for Christian marriages to be a reflection of Your love for humanity. May the words in this book plant seeds in the heart of everyone who reads it. That they may grow in love, patience, kindness and understanding with their mate and live out Your glorious plan for

their marriage. In the name of Jesus, Amen.

INDEX OF PRAYERS FOR HUSBANDS & WIVES

The following index of Scriptures is for you and your husband to meditate on and pray from together. You may not be able to pray together every day in the beginning. To start, set a time once a week to pray together.

Numbers 30:2 If a man makes a vow to the Lord, or swears an oath to bind himself by some agreement, he shall not break his word; he shall do according to all that proceeds out of his mouth.

Psalm 128:3 Your wife shall be like a fruitful vine in the very heart of your house, your children like olive plants all around your table.

Proverbs 18:22 He who find a wife finds a good thing, and obtains favor from the Lord.

Proverbs 28:13 He who covers his sins will not prosper, but whoever confesses and forsakes them will have mercy.

Proverbs 31:28-29 Her children rise up and call her blessed; her husband also, and he praises her: "Many daughters have done well, but you excel them all."

Song of Solomon 1:2 Let him kiss me with the kisses of his mouth – for your love is better than wine.

Song of Solomon 4:7; 9-10 You are fair my love and there is no spot in you. You have ravished my heart with one look of your eyes, how much better than wine is your love and the scent of your perfumes than all spices.

Song of Solomon 5:16 His mouth is most sweet, yes he is altogether lovely. This is my beloved and this is my friend.

Song of Solomon 7:10 I am my beloved's and his desire is toward me.

Song of Solomon 8:7 Many waters cannot quench love, nor can the floods drown it. If a man would give for love all the wealth of his house, it would be utterly despised.

Amos 3:3 Can two walk together, unless they are agreed?

Matthew 7:1-2 Judge not, that you be not judged. For with what judgment you judge, you will be judged; and with the measure you use, it will be measured back to you.

Matthew 18:19-20 Again I say to you if two or you agree on earth concerning anything that they ask, it will be done for them by My Father in heaven. For where two or three are gather together in My name, I am there in the midst of them.

Luke 16:18 Whoever divorces his wife, and marries another, commits adultery; and whoever marries her who is divorced from her husband commits adultery.

John 14:13 And whatever you ask in My name, that I will do, that the Father may be glorified in the Son.

Romans 10:17 So then faith comes by hearing, and hearing by the word of God.

Romans 12:19-21 Beloved, do not avenge yourselves, but rather give place to wrath; for it is written, "Vengeance is Mine, I will repay," says the Lord. Therefore "If your enemy is hungry, feed him; if he is thirsty, give him drink; for in doing so you will heap coals of fires on his head." Do not be overcome by evil, but overcome evil with good.

1 Corinthians 1:10 Now I plead with you, brethren, by the name of our Lord Jesus Christ, that you all speak the same thing, and that there be no divisions among you, but that you be perfectly joined together in the same mind and in the same judgment.

1 Corinthians 7: 10 Now to the married I command, yet not I but

the Lord: A wife is not to depart from her husband. But even if she does depart, let her remain unmarried or be reconciled to her husband. And a husband is not to divorce his wife.

1 Corinthians 7:14 For the unbelieving husband is sanctified by his wife, and the unbelieving wife is sanctified by the husband; otherwise your children would be unclean, but now they are holy.

Ephesians 4:29 Let no corrupt word proceed out of your mouth, but what is good for necessary edification, that it may impart grace to the hearers.

Ephesians 5:22 Wives, submit to your own husbands, as to the Lord

Ephesians 5:24 Therefore just as the church is subject to Christ, so let the wives be to their own husbands in everything.

Ephesians 5:25 Husbands, love your wives, even as Christ also loved the church, and gave Himself for it.

Ephesians 5:28-29 So husbands ought to love their own wives as their own bodies; he who loves his wife loves himself. For no one ever hated his own flesh, bur nourishes and cherishes it, just as the Lord does the church.

Ephesians 5:33 Nevertheless let each one of you in particular so love his own wife as himself, and let the wife see that she respects her husband.

Colossians 3:19 Husbands, love your wives and do not be bitter toward them.

Colossians 3:23 And whatever you do, do it heartily, as to the Lord and not to men.

1 Thessalonians 5:16-18 Rejoice always, pray without ceasing, in everything give thanks; for this is the will of God in Christ Jesus for you.

Titus 2:4-5 That they may admonish the young women to love their husbands, to love their children, to be discreet, chaste, homemakers, good, obedient to their own husbands, that the word of God may not be blasphemed.

1 Peter 3:1 Wives, likewise, be submissive to your own husbands; that even if some do not obey the word, they without a word, may be won by the conduct of their wives.

1 Peter 3:7 Husbands, likewise, dwell with them with understanding, giving honor to the wife, as unto the weaker vessel, and as being heirs together of the grace of life; that your prayers may not be hindered.

1 John 3:16 By this we know love, because He laid down His life for us. And we also out to lay down our lives for the brethren.

ABOUT THE AUTHOR

Nicole Denise Perkins McLaughlin began writing in the seventh grade and has poems published in journals and anthologies. She received an Honorable Mention in the Writer's Digest 2000 writing competition for her stage play script Harlem Renaissance.

She received her BA in Theater from Florida A&M University. Nicole spent two seasons as the Managing Director of The Smithsonian Associates Discovery Theater for Children.

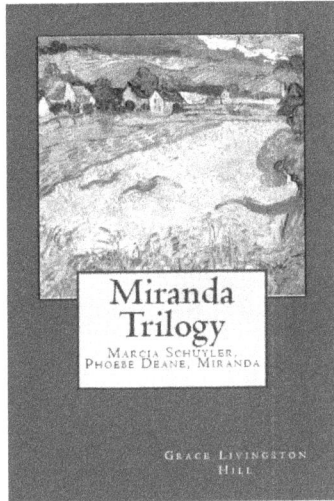

Miranda
Trilogy
MARCIA SCHUYLER,
PHOEBE DEANE, MIRANDA

GRACE LIVINGSTON
HILL

Miranda Trilogy

By

Grace Livingston Hill

ISBN: 978-1-62943-003-4

This anthology consists of Marcia Schuyler, Phoebe Deane and
Miranda.
(3 Books in 1)

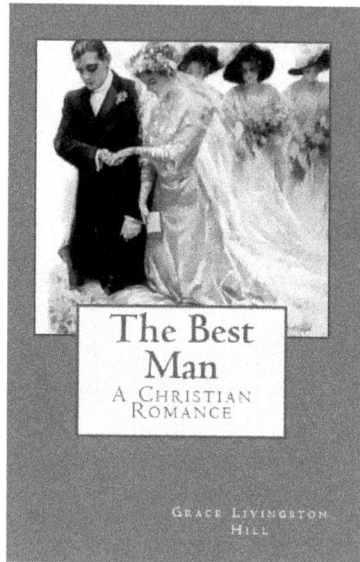

The Best Man (A Christian Romance)

By: Grace Livingston Hill

ISBN: 978-1-62943-007-2

The story is about the love between Celia Hathaway and Cyril Gordon. Cyril Gordon is a handsome Secret Service Agent who stumbles in upon a wedding ceremony while he is being chased by his pursuers. He is being forced to walk down the aisle as the best man as he was being mistaken by the people in the church. But to his surprise, he was not the best man, but the groom!

Fifty Shakes
of
Matrimony

Seine Emerald

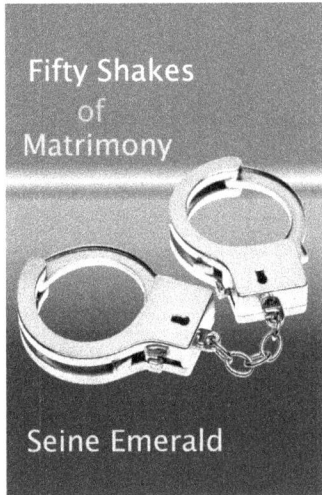

Fifty Shakes of Matrimony
By
Seine Emerald

ISBN: 978-1629430010

A Contemporary Romance

A Tale of Love, betrayal, forgiveness and Hope

Seine is outgoing, bright and confident. She finds success as a writer and managed to sell a screenplay to a major TV network.

The fictionalized story is based on her own experiences in emotional affair with a younger married man in her church.

While she is happy with her career growth, She has her world rocked when her secret is exposed.

Members of the church found out her affair with the "man". And hence she is being kicked out of the church.

Will she release herself from the bondage of guilt? or remain bound by guilt?

Will she able to reconcile with her husband?

Will the power of forgiveness set her free?

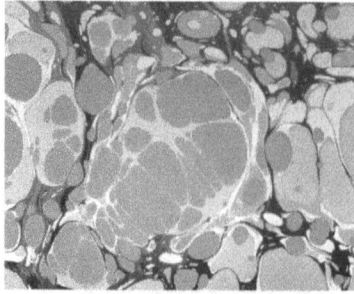

THE WHEELS OF TIME

FLORENCE L. BARCLAY

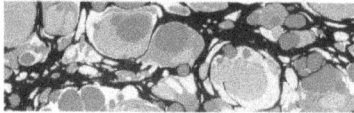

The Wheels of Time

By

Florence L. Barclay

ISBN:978-1491064948

A Charmingly touching Story

It is a prequel to The Rosary.

Dr. Deryck Brand stood, with his hand on the door-knob, looking back into his wife's boudoir.

There was nothing in that room suggestive of town or of town life and work--delicate green and white, a mossy carpet, masses of spring flowers; cool, soft, noiseless, fragrant.

Standing in the doorway, the doctor could hear the agitated clang of the street-door bell, Stoddart crossing the hall, the opening and closing of the door, and Stoddart's subdued and sympathetic voice saying: "Step this way, please." A heavy, depressed foot, or an anxious, hurried one...

www.ingramcontent.com/pod-product-compliance
Lightning Source LLC
Chambersburg PA
CBHW062027040426

42447CB00010B/2168